MW00787287

Building Character Through Sports

Transitioning from Team Sports to Team Business

"How Playing Sports Teaches Us to Win in Business and Life"

Leman "Buzy" Rosenberg

All rights reserved.

Copyright ©2005 by Leman Rosenberg

ISBN 0-9759818-4-6

Published and distributed by:
High-Pitched Hum Publishing
321 15th Street North
Jacksonville Beach, FL 32250

Contact Leman Rosenberg at **www.buzyrosenberg.com**
No part of this book may be reproduced or transmitted in any form
or means, electronic or mechanical, including photocopying,
recording, or by any information storage and retrieval system,
without permission in writing from the publisher.

Ross,

Coachable people have a chance to reach their full potential. Winning is your choice.

Buzz Rabey

"Thank you to the moms, dads, teachers and coaches who give of your time to motivate others by having a positive attitude and by teaching the winning habits it takes to be successful."

Table of Contents

Introduction

*"At the end of the day there are
many exceptions to every rule."*

"Building Character Through Sports" is a book about learning
how to win along the way when all is said and done. If I had the
power, every child would have the opportunity to play team sports.
The experiences and winning habits learned participating in sports
are the reasons many people are winners in life and business.
Young people do not realize the positive influence of sport until
they get older and look back at the reasons they become successful
people. The topics in this book center on how mentors and coaches
influence and teach the winning habits learned by participating in
team sports. My story was not supposed to happen. How many 5
feet 8.5 inch defensive backs have started in Division 1 football?
Add that question to my lack of great speed, my last name being
Rosenberg and the odds of a guy like me playing football in the
SEC are greater than winning the lottery. Never believe people
that tell you "You Can't" because you are the only one who has
that right. I was a "B" football player who was able to attain ALL
SEC honors my sophomore and junior years and set one NCAA
punt return record and several University of Georgia punt return
records that still stand today. The "Yes I can" attitude and the

focus on leadership is illustrated throughout this book and hopefully teaches the winning habits learned playing sports are important for any person's success. There are many exceptions to every rule and you might be that exception. Do not go through life without trying and continuously challenging life's obstacles because at the end of the day, it is better to have tried and lost than to have never tried. At the end of the day, the things people measure are not as important as the things people do not measure. No person can measure one's will to win, one's work ethic, one's competitive drive, one's team driven philosophy, one's ability to get their adrenalin going to do unreal things both physically and mentally. When a person stays within bounds and takes advantage of the good things sports has to offer, his or her future success in business and life is unlimited.

The Purpose

Some people are luckier than others and the influence of four Hall of Fame football coaches growing up has made a big difference in my life. Coach Bob Blackwell was the grandfather of Pop Warner football in Atlanta and was named the Pop Warner coach of the year several times during his 25-year span of coaching. Coach Waymen Creel was named the High School National Coach of the Year in 1977 and won 315 football games before he died early in life of a heart attack at 64 years old. He is one of 16 coaches named to the Georgia High School Hall of Fame. Coach Erk Russell won 4 college national championships in the 80's. One as a Defensive Coordinator at the University of Georgia in 1980 and three as the Head Coach and Athletic Director at Georgia Southern from 1983 through 1989. Under Coach Russell's leadership the Bulldogs led the SEC in scoring defense in 1967 and 1977 and finished 2nd in the nation in scoring defense in 1978 and 1979. Coach Russell started the football program at

Georgia Southern in 1981 and built the best Division I AA football program of the 80's.

Coach Vince Dooley is a legend at the University of Georgia. He won six SEC championships and one national championship. His record was 201 wins – 77 losses – 10 ties. In 25 years of coaching, he took his teams to 20 bowl appearances. The lessons taught by these four great leaders will be shared through out this book as the experiences I've had are told.

I am thankful God gave me enough athletic ability and mental toughness to play sports, not because of the accolades, not because people know who we are, not because an athlete is the big man on campus, but because through playing sports some great leaders had a positive influence on my life.

The purpose in writing this book is to give back some of what has been given to me and to show the positive life long influence participating in sports has on 99% of athletes. For every player or coach that goes out of bounds and places a black eye on the sport he participates in, there are thousands of people that stay within bounds and learn or teach the winning habits it takes to be successful in life and business.

Chapter One

Challenges in The 60's
Diversity and Sports

The late 1960's was a time of great challenge and change in America and in my hometown of Atlanta, Georgia. I was a young boy growing into a young man during this decade. Looking back on this time in history makes me proud of the people that helped make the transition to integration easier.

Competition in sports was changing for both the white and black athletes. For the first time white and black teams were given the opportunity to compete against each other. Neither race had any idea how they would fare. Fortunately, for both, stereotypes were changing.

I was a participant in some of the first football games played between predominately black football teams and predominately white football teams. These events brought our communities together and I hope that in some way I helped with the transition. The games were very competitive and a whole lot of fun. Classrooms faced challenges as students from various backgrounds came together. Attitudes needed to be changed. If you haven't already seen the movie *"REMEMBER THE TITANS"*, please do so. It is a true story about integration in Virginia. I saw this movie and it brought back memories and gave me chills. Life in America was changing.

I remember thinking in the 1960's that one-day folks would look back and talk about the 60's the same way we were looking back and talking about past decades. What would the future bring and how would things change?

The athletic field has always been a good place to meet people. Our Northside High varsity basketball team won the city championship in my sophomore year by beating Carver High. Both Carver and Northside had the highest respect for each other. The same year, Carver beat Northside for the State Championship. We also split regular season games with both teams winning one game. These competitions were the beginning of ethnic diversity in the South.

A few years later, our Northside High football team and the Archer High football team played each other late in the season and the game was decided by a "fourth and one" goal line stand by the Archer team. Archer went on to play in the city championship. The early contests between the races were competitive. I think it all came down to the fact that neither group of people had the mental advantage in those days. Both groups grew up playing in the playground. Attitude always makes the difference in winning or losing.

In the 1960's, all young people were out playing in their neighborhoods. They were not sitting in their house watching TV or playing video games. Both races had a "Yes I can" attitude. The family played a more important part for all people with both the father and mother present for a secure childhood.

The students who integrated Northside High in the 60's did fine in school. I never noticed any difference between the black students and the white student's ability to get through Northside. The attitude of the black students was "Yes I can" do this. Most people wanted integration to be a smooth transition. The experiences had a big influence on all of us who were there.

Two black women influenced my life significantly. Martha helped raise me from birth until I was 9 years old and was my second mom. Martha's husband "Bubba" taught me how to catch and throw a football. He was a big, strong man standing over 6 ft tall and weighing well over 200lbs. He was a solid man who loved children. Bubba would have been a professional athlete had he come up in today's era. The experience of knowing Bubba at an early age was the primary reason I was able to compete in high school at the level I did. I had already seen and played with a man a lot bigger and stronger than any kid I would ever play against. Bubba was a lot like my own dad. He was a caring, loving person centered on integrity who loved teaching me how to catch a football. My experience with black people in the 1960's was and is the reason I know the difference between the natural ability of all people in all areas of life is minimal if at all. Martha had a positive influence on me as a young man. She was with my sisters and me every day. If we did something wrong, she would discipline us. When I first began playing football at Fritz Orr camp at 9 years old, it was Martha that got stuck with the job of driving me to practice. Martha would drive me to practice and I would cry the whole way because I did not want to play tackle football as a young 9-year-old boy. Martha told me recently, after dropping me off for football, she would drive down the street and start crying, herself. She didn't like leaving me at football practice because she knew I didn't want to play. The love Martha showed all of the Rosenberg family has been a positive influence throughout life. Through Martha's influence, we learned a lot. She taught us that people have the same human nature regardless of the differences in their culture.

Cora was my third mom. From nine years old through high school, Cora helped raise us. As a young boy, I would go with

Cora to her home to play with the kids in her neighborhood. I never thought myself any different and because of my passion for sports, I was readily accepted. Cora pushed me to be the best in every sport. She never missed any of my high school football games. Most folks thought Cora was my real mom. Being a good leaper and quick, it was always a compliment when folks would compare my athletic ability with other top athletes.

The support and pride in Cora's eyes when she would talk to others about her boy motivated me more than she or I, at the time could know. The positive support from Cora gave me the confidence needed to compete competitively in the 60's. Living with Cora every day gave me the right attitude that otherwise, I might not have had.

Martha, Bubba and Buzy

Throughout my athletic career, because of my mentality, influenced to a great degree by my three mother figures, I played better when competing against the best athletes. I was never intimidated by anybody. Competition in business or sports will always be to compete from within and to always challenge yourself. If a 100% effort is given, one is a winner regardless of the score.

We are all a summation of every experience we have in our life. I did not know then that the experiences of being loved by Martha, Cora and Bubba would have an everlasting impression on me. We all should be ethnically diverse and appreciate people who possess the qualities we think are important to be successful in life. I learned we are different yet we are so very much alike.

Life's Lessons Learned through the Influence of Sport

1. The natural athletic ability and the natural aptitude of all people is not what today's American society would have you think.
2. Life in America will always be changing.
3. Attitude in sports, business or life will always make the difference in winning and losing.
4. Mutual respect is a powerful habit to be centered on and the only long-term respect is mutual respect.
5. It is the heart, soul and mind that define a person.
6. Environment does have a lasting effect on all of us.
7. To be the best, one must compete against the best.
8. People do have different cultures but all people have the same basic human nature.

Chapter Two

Building Character at an Early Age
Leadership

Good leaders motivate people to go places they might never go. Good leaders encourage people to try things they might not ever try. They teach people to overachieve. Leadership is influenced and cannot be learned in a day, it takes years to learn to be a good leader.

The experiences illustrated in this chapter are all positive because some people are luckier than others. Two people often have the same ability and one will become successful and one will be a failure. We all come upon crossroads in life and the decisions we make determine our success or failure. Good leadership always makes the difference. The following shows how influence from mentors and coaches make the long-term difference.

"Stay within bounds"

My father has always been the most important mentor of my life. When I was seven years old, he took me up the street to play touch football with the older kids in the neighborhood. He told me it was time for me to begin competing with other children. I was nervous and scared, but I did have dad at my side so I was willing to give it a shot. I wanted to throw and catch a football with the neighborhood kids. As we were walking up the street, dad told me, "Buzy, have fun and try not to be scared." I did not reply because I was scared. Looking back, this was the first time I ever felt adrenalin in relationship to sports competition. We got to the field where the kids were playing and dad asked Forest Myers, the oldest kid (11 yrs old), if I could play on one of the teams. Forest told dad I was small and might get hurt. He replied, "Buzy won't get hurt." They put me at center to hike the ball. Forest reluctantly let me play on his team because dad was an adult and he had to.

Every kid on my team was talking but the only thing said to me was hike the ball on one. I did not realize that day; I would need to overachieve during my entire athletic career to earn recognition because off the field I did not look the part. I was on a team but no one paid any attention to me. As we walked home, dad asked me, "Did you have fun?" I told him that I had fun but asked, "Why didn't I get the ball thrown to me at least one time?" He told me, "Son, you are a good athlete and you can catch and run better than most of the older kids. You will have to ask the big kids to throw the ball to you if you want it to happen." The lesson he was trying to teach me was, do not expect others to give you anything; if you want something ask for it. When we got home I gave dad a hug and forgot about playing football.

Three days later dad came home from work again to take me up the street to play football. As we were walking to the playing field he told me to ask Forest to throw me a pass and to tell Forest, if I dropped it, I would not ask him again. I was shy and did not want to ask this question. Leave it up to dad because father knows best. In the middle of playing a very important game (to us it was important), he walks over to the huddle and tells Forest to throw me the ball. Forest reluctantly said, "Yes, sir." The rest is history; I ran down the field as fast as my legs would let me run, Forest threw the ball as far as he could and I caught it and scored a touchdown. It was my first touchdown and I was happy. But not as happy or proud as my dad. Forest looked at dad and said; "Mr. Rosenberg, Buzy can play." After catching that ball, Forest threw several more passes to me that day and I caught every one of them. Dad and I were walking home when he looked at me and said, "You will be a good football player, but because of your size, you will always have to overacheive when given the chance." I had just scored my first touchdown and was on cloud nine and thought I was pretty good, so I did not understand the wisdom of my father on that day. The bigger older kids came to get me to play from that day on. All kids need dad's positive support.

A lesson learned at a young age

At 9 years old, dad thought it was time for me to play real football with pads on. If dad said it was time to play real football, then I was going to give it a shot. Fritz Orr's camp had a football team and dad signed me up to play. It was a weird experience. My first practice was not good. The coach was not nice to me and I got intimidated. I was not an impressive football player with my pads hanging off my body and I was not confident in my ability. I got home sick because dad didn't make practice. I sat in the bushes crying. I heard the coach say, "Let the crybaby cry, if he doesn't want to play, let him cry." Cry I did because I did not want to play football and told my dad I didn't want to play. Dad knew if he let me quit that I might always look for the easy way out so he told me quitting is not an option and would never be an option. I was not happy and did not want to play.

The next practice, dad showed up to watch us play and asked the coach to let me run the football. What happens next is really weird. I ran for a touchdown every time I touched the ball. I was quick and the kids had a hard time touching me and I was pretty tough as well. However, after running for several touchdowns, I ran back to sit in the bushes and cry. Like most kids, I was sensitive and did not like the coach calling me a crybaby. The coach had hurt my feelings and I thought he did not like me. I was lucky the camp only lasted 2 weeks because my dad made me show up every day for practice. He taught me the lesson that I was not ever going to be a quitter. The coach was not a bad guy but I was young and took what he said personally. Coaches should be careful how they handle kids because with a lesser father, I might have quit and learned to quit instead of that quitting would never be an option. Thanks again dad for always having my best interest at heart.

I never thought I would grow up to play high school or college football. Thank God dad always told me I can do anything I want to do. The only limits any person has is the limits that person places on themselves.

"Yes I can" beats "No I can't" every time

"Buzy's a good little football player, but he will never have the size to play for Georgia."

At 12 years old, I was attending a Georgia football game with dad when he was telling two men sitting next to us a story about what happened in a Pop Warner football game just a few days earlier. I was a lucky kid to be able to play football for the legendary Bob Blackwell and the Buckhead Red Devils. We just won the State Championship and I faked a punt and ran 70 yards for a touchdown late in the 2nd quarter to help our team win the game against the Waycross All Stars by a score of 13 to 7. These two gentlemen listened to my proud dad talk about his little boy and then told both dad and myself, "Buzy might be a good Pop Warner player, but he will never have the size to get on the University of Georgia football field." The comment hurt but it became a turning point in the goals I set for myself. For the first time in my life I wanted to play football for the University of Georgia and make those two men eat their words. I have learned the people who tell others what they cannot do are not successful people and definitely not good leaders.

After returning the first punt ever punted to me in a college football game for a 62 yard touchdown, my first thought was, "Where are those two men who said I was too small and would never be big enough to play for Georgia." This was the beginning of my football career, but the challenges of playing college football and a try-out to play professional football were in my future.

> *"People who criticize usually talk about what they wish they could do. So, I never paid much attention to critics about anything negative."*
> *The Soul of a Butterfly*
> *Muhammad Ali*

Coach Blackwell

At 12 years of age and standing less than 5 ft tall and 94 lbs, my father put me in the back of his car and drove me to Bagley Park in the Buckhead area of Atlanta to try out for football. Dad forgot to tell me this football team was named the Buckhead Red Devils and they were reputedly the best Pop Warner football team in America. He also did not mention the boys I would be playing against would be 13 years old and I would have to win a position on the team. The coach was Bob Blackwell who would become the grandfather of Pop Warner football in Atlanta and who, a few years earlier, had been named the National Pop Warner coach of the year.

This challenge was my first opportunity to compete in sports at a high level. I was intimidated the first couple of days practicing in shorts with the older, bigger, better built kids. I had skinny legs and always had a little fat around my middle (even as I got older, I was never considered "built"). The question was: would I be able to compete at this level?

Every player touched by Coach Blackwell became a better person. The first day we practiced in pads, I made a nice hit on one of the older, better athletes. The way Coach Blackwell reacted one might have thought I made the saving tackle to win the Super Bowl. You see, Coach Blackwell was a master motivator, lucky for me. He picked out the smallest player. I am sure he selected the one he thought might not make the team, to set an example of something good and to inspire a reaction from the bigger, better and older athletes. He also, as I learned later in life from Coach himself, wanted to challenge his best players every chance he got by elevating the play of his second and third team players, which he thought I would be. He said the results were a win – win situation. Every player on his team got better with this approach to coaching and every kid began to think "Yes I can."

I thought coach liked my play and my confidence skyrocketed. I made the team; played first string and the Red Devils went undefeated and won another National Championship. Because of Coach Blackwell's support and encouragement, I learned to become a competitor and in the end, an overachiever. Coach taught his players the power of "Yes I can." A lesson for all to learn.

Coach Blackwell was a master at making everybody on the team better and particularly the lesser players. He taught us that any person who gives 100% is a winner. He taught us that we win as a team and we lose as a team. He was a stickler for learning and practicing the fundamentals of the game. He taught that every player on the team was a very important part of the team. He was a great motivator and a clear communicator. The trust that we all had for Coach Blackwell was a big reason for our success. Little did we know the habits it takes to be successful in business and happy in life began the day we met Bob Blackwell.

The ultimate compliment given to me by Coach Blackwell came at the end of the season when our undefeated 12-year old Pop Warner team played the Waycross All Stars. Waycross had a great Pop Warner football team. We were losing by a touchdown with only a few seconds left in the first half. We had a 4th down and long situation on our own 30-yard line. Coach Blackwell called a time out and brought the entire team to the sideline. He looked at me and said, "Buzy, fake the punt and run for a TD. Don't stop running until you get to the end zone and Buzy, I believe in you." I got back in punt formation, faked the punt, and made the best run of my entire career. I ran to my right, broke free and had only the other team's punt returner to beat. I made a dip and go move on the defensive player and ran to the end zone for the score 70 yards later. When people believe in you, you do unreal things and Coach believed in me. The best play I ever made was in Pop Warner football in Waycross, Georgia, not in high school, not in college but as a 12-year-old boy. Coach Blackwell and I have relived that run many times with each other. We all were very lucky kids to have been touched by Coach Blackwell. We did go on to win the State Championship game by a score of 13 to 7.   .

"I'm looking for a lot of men with an infinite
capacity for not knowing what can't be done"
Henry Ford

The most influential person in most Northside High Football player's lives was Coach Wayman Creel. "We can measure the score at the end of the game, but we cannot measure the effort it took prior to the game or during the game to win." This was one of Coach Creel's greater life lessons.

Staff Photo—Charles Bennett
WAYMAN CREEL (R), STAN GANN GIVE QUARTERBACK BUZ ROSENBERG A DRINK
Gann Returns to Northside and Creel Has Visions of Returning to Glory Days

At 13 years of age and in the eighth grade, I decided to play football for my new school, Northside High. Moving away from Coach Blackwell was a tough decision to make because I loved Coach and for the only time in my life, I would have been one of the bigger kids on the Buckhead Red Devils at 120 lbs. But I wanted to compete with the big boys so I opted to play on the Northside High eighth grade team. I played quarterback and defensive safety. We all met Coach Waymen Creel as eighth grade athletes.

Coach Creel was renowned as one of the best high school coaches to ever come out of the state of Georgia. He was honored as the National High School Coach of the Year in 1977. His final record was 315 wins – 105 losses – 12 ties and is one of only 5 high school coaches in the state of Georgia to win over 300 games.

Coach had a 38-year coaching career and was twice appointed the President of the Georgia Athletic Coaches Association. Today he is one of only 16 coaches that have been honored as a Georgia High School Coach Hall of Fame member. What a great experience to move from the best Pop Warner program and coach in America to the best high school program in America led by a man that in the future would become a second father to most of us and a great mentor for life.

The habits to be successful in business and happy in life that were taught at 12 years old by the best Pop Warner coach in America were now going to be taught by a man who I would come to consider the best mentor in my life outside of my father. Coach Creel taught us the same winning habits for success that Coach Blackwell taught. The best time of my life and the most fun I ever had was playing high school football during integration in the city of Atlanta, Georgia.

A little additional information to re-enforce the power of a positive "Yes I can" attitude. Our eighth grade basketball team went 18 wins and 0 losses. I was 5 ft 2 inches tall and could jump up and touch a 10 ft basketball rim. I worked at jumping because at a young age, I was aware my height would be a weakness if I did not play BIG. God gives us our height and our weight but our work ethic, our competitive spirit, our attitude and good leadership determine how big we will play. The goal should always be to respect all competitors and to strive to earn the respect of your competitors.

My first experience playing directly for Coach Creel was in the 10th grade at 15 years old. Coach Creel did a great job coaching a group of average athletes up to become a good football team. Our high school team went 10 wins and 1 loss with the lone loss coming in the Milk Bowl while playing for the city championship. We were ranked number 2 in the state but got upset by Brown High. I do think we had the best team in the state that year but because of this upset, we will never know. I started at flanker and was the 2nd team quarterback as a 10th grader. My junior year was the year Coach Creel and I began to develop our lifetime love and respect for each other. Coach was a strong disciplinarian and did not let any of us get away with anything. We couldn't go out of bounds because coach would stop us before we started. Coach would often call me in to his office and check to make sure my hair was cut to his standards and most of the time it wasn't so he would pull the scissors out and cut my bangs. I actually looked forward to coach cutting my hair and appreciated him not making me special in any way. Most kids want discipline. We had a good football team but not a great one. Our record was 7 wins and three losses. My senior year Coach Creel took another group of average athletes and almost won the city championship and then maybe the state. Our only loss was to Archer High by a few points. Competing with Archer for the District Championship was the first time Jerome Nelloms, Archer High School's great running back, and I met. Northside High was always ready to play both mentally and physically. We learned what it takes to get prepared to be successful for any of life's challenges playing football for Coach Creel.

Coach Creel was a disciplinarian and instilled great confidence in his football players. He could beat yours with his and his with yours. In other words, Coach Creel won by coaching the fundamentals of the game and instilling in all his players the "Yes I can" attitude because he never had the best athletes when I played for him.

Creel taught that any person who gives 100% is a winner. He mirrored Coach Blackwell's philosophy. He taught us, we win as a team and we lose as a team. He was a stickler for learning and practicing the fundamentals of the game. He taught that every player on the team was an important part of the team. He was a great motivator and a clear communicator. The discipline that he instilled in all of us has lasted our lifetime. The trust that we all had for Coach Creel was a big reason for our success. His influence has lasted a lifetime for many of the kids that attended Northside High.

Coach Creel taught that one's mental attitude is the most important part of any person's success. The following comment motivated me to try things I might not have ever tried and go places I might not have ever gone. Coach Creel once said, "Buzy's strength and will to compete are not measurable." I asked Coach what he meant by what he said. He told me, some people have a winner's attitude and both their will to compete and their strength does not come from their physical being. It comes from their mental ability and cannot be measured. He said, "There are no limits to what a person can do if he has the right attitude and believes he can."

He showed me film of when I ran faster than I can run to score a touchdown or catch a faster runner from behind. This statement motivated and taught me more than I could ever measure. It gave me the confidence needed to compete at a high level. This lesson should be taught and learned by all people. We have many young athletes who will overachieve if they are taught this lesson.

#14, a 9.9 second 100 yard dash sprinter, chasing a 10.4 sprinter, but the will to compete and the fear of defeat motivated this 70 yard touchdown

The philosophy of the book "The 7 Habits of Highly Effective People" was learned from men like Coach Blackwell and Coach Creel. Coach Creel was of Indian decent and one of the best-conditioned men I have ever known. It is enlightening to think back and realize that I was playing football for an American Indian. I had a Jewish father and a Mormon mother. We, my team and I, were competing in the first white vs. black football games. I did not realize these things until I began to write this book. Some people in the 60's were further along than today's society would have you believe.

Coach Creel died in 1990 riding a bike during a work out. He was 64 years old and still in great shape. He went out the way he wanted to go out. Every kid that was ever touched by Waymen Creel is better today because of it.

Life's Lessons Learned From Sports Influence

1. Sport Leadership builds character at a young age that will last a life-time.
2. The smaller one is physically, the bigger one must be mentally.
3. A "Yes I can" attitude creates a winner.
4. Winning Business practices (Habits and Attitudes) are learned playing sports at a very young age.
5. Quitting should never be an option.
6. Discipline is key to any person's long term success.
7. Some folks are luckier than others.
8. The things we measure are not as important as the things we do not measure.
9. Do not expect others to give you anything, if you want something, ask for it.

Chapter Three

Mutual Respect

For most of us, high school athletics bring back fun memories. We are easily influenced in high school and we change on a daily basis. Our bodies and our minds are beginning to mature into a young man or woman. This chapter outlines high school football during the first days of integration in Atlanta Georgia in the 1960's. The following are lessons learned playing sports in high school.

In retrospect, the best memories of my life were on Friday or Saturday nights playing football for Waymen Creel and Northside High at Cheney or Grady stadium in 1966, 67, and 68. You would have had to be present at these games to feel the excitement and the energy as the first games between the best predominately white football teams and the best predominantly black football teams were played.

The athletes had great respect for each other. The fact we had never competed against each other made all of us a little scared of the unknown. Neither team had an advantage of confidence, experience or anything else.

I did realize early in these competitions the same advantage Coach Creel gave our Northside High team playing against the white teams, he gave us playing against the black teams. Coach

Creel often was the difference in winning or losing any football game.

Having a competitive nature encouraged the student body of the opposing schools to both respect and want to hurt me at the same time. Competing with the best athletes has always been important and now that we were integrated, we all got to play against all the best athletes. Challenging yourself to be the best is true competition. My reputation as a person that loved to compete and expected to win every time I stepped on the field earned me the respect I wanted and always gave to my competition. Being aggressive was not an option because both Martha and Cora told me not to let anyone intimidate me. Cora was at every game to make sure I competed hard. The energy I got from the student body of the opposing teams made me play better. Earning respect not only from the opposing ball players but also from the opposing student body was the ultimate challenge and goal. Making a big hit was more important than making a long run. People do enjoy doing things most folks think they cannot do.

"Be sure you can back up what you say"

Each road game became a party with the student body of our competitors rocking and rolling in the stands the entire night. The show of respect was memorable. It was my goal to give these fans exactly what they came to see. Talking with the best talkers was easy and natural. During one game, we received the kick off and ran it back to around the 28 yard line. The entire other team was beating on their pads and yelling that they were going to hurt me. When I looked into my team's wide eyes and saw my teammates concern, I laughed and called a play for me to run the ball at the biggest, baddest player on the defensive line and one of the best players in the city. After we walked up to the line of scrimmage and both teams got down in their stance ready for battle, I left my quarterback position from underneath the center and walked over to the big guy we were going to run the play at and said, "Get ready big guy, we are coming right at you and my little butt is going to run over you." We ran the play for about 8 yards. I helped the big guy up and did not say a word but neither did he. We had earned each other's respect. It is fun to compete against different styles of competition. After the play, all of the players on my team were laughing at me. I asked, "Are you still concerned?" and got a big smile from everybody. The only response to the smiles was "let's win this game." Leading by example is a lesson learned playing sports that should become a winning habit used for business and life.

The word spread that I had told one of the strongest and best defensive lineman in the city to look out because I was coming his way and was going to run over him. These first integrated games were fun for both races. I was not the best football player on the field but I had been taught, don't ever be intimidated, don't ever back down, make your competition earn everything they get and if you win or lose, live with it.

We won a lot of these games and when the games were over, we loved the post game hugs, handshakes and friendships. The mutual respect we developed with our competitors was commendable. I thank God often that he allowed me to have a diverse upbringing and a competitive spirit so when this changing time of integration took place, I could be a part of it and hopefully help to move through integration more smoothly.

The lessons we all learned playing football in high school last a lifetime. The following are a few examples of games in high school that taught lessons still practiced today and most of us have these same experiences to learn from.

The Price High game was played during the worst weather imaginable. It was 35 degrees and had rained all day. We played the game under the lights at night and the field was wet. It took both teams one quarter to get started. I finally broke a long run and remember one of the opposing players commenting, "I would have got you but I just can't run in this weather." I replied "If you start running, maybe you will warm up." I should never have said that. He did start running. We were up 33 to 7 at the end of the 3rd quarter but what a 4th quarter. The player I told, "You should start running" really started to run. He scored 3 TDS in the 4th quarter and we escaped with a win only because time ran out. He came up to me at the end of the game and said, "Thank you for motivating me to run." We both smiled and gave each other a hug. Sometimes it is better to keep your mouth shut but having fun along the way is most important.

The Archer High game was the best and most competitive high school game I played in. We played each other late in the year to determine the team that would represent our region in the state playoffs. We had a competitive game with both teams playing their hearts out. It came down to a 4th and less than 1 yard with our team about to score late in the game. We ran a power I formation and tried to dive our halfback up the middle to score and go ahead. Archer made a great play and stopped us from scoring. I want to salute the Archer players for a job well done. It hurt a lot, but all of the kids on our team gave their best effort and that is always all that can ever be expected.

It was very exciting to play in front of the loud crowd at Archer High. The Archer band was one of, if not the best, band in the city and they were really into this big game. I ran faster than I could run in returning a punt, 65 yards for a score. Archer played their best game of the year and they deserve credit for rising to the occasion and beating a very good team. We made some good plays but when it counted the most, we did not produce and Archer did. I love the fact that sports are honest and so real. Archer beat us fair and square. The only thing the players on the Northside High team could do was to learn from the loss and get better because of it.

We all learn a lot more from losing than winning. Losing hurts so much and to keep from hurting often, it is very important to learn from losing and get better. The lesson learned in this loss was, "better focus and concentration when we had the opportunity to put this game away, would have changed the outcome."

The Douglas High game was the last game of my high school career and scoring 5 touchdowns in this game is a result of being focused more than usual. We had lost to Archer and losing again was not an option. As a team, we ran a punt return for a TD, a pass interception was returned for a TD, and a TD pass was thrown. I ran from my QB position for a touchdown, and then I ran for another TD from the half back position. The best thing about the game was that the Archer High players were waiting to play the next game and were in the end zone watching Northside High beat Douglas by a large margin. Every time we scored a TD they clapped with appreciation. The respect we had for each other was super.

What a way to go out. It was satisfying to play our personal best game the last game of our high school careers. Mental focus is any person's or team's best asset.

Friends are friends and color should never be a barrier

The 1960's were "the age of Aquarius" and social change was happening right before our eyes. As we have seen and experienced over the last 35 or 40 years, change takes time.

Jerome Nelloms, the #1 black star athlete in Atlanta high school football back in the day, often invited me to come to his neighborhood to play touch football. We played on the Morris Brown, Morehouse and Clark campuses. The first time Jerome asked me to come over, my only question was, "Will I be ok?" Jerome responded, "Folks will have to go through me to get to you, Buzy and nobody is going through me." I was a little apprehensive but I wanted to compete, so I got in my mom's car without telling her where I was going and proceeded to do what I wanted to do.

The mutual respect we had for each other and the unbelievable competition even playing touch football will never be forgotten. Every player on the field was a strong competitor. I often think about those fun days. There is always one thought that comes to mind. Why could I go to their neighborhood and be respected but they could not come to my neighborhood and receive the same respect? The truth is I did not have the strength of character to go against what in those days were the social barriers and invite a black friend to my neighborhood.

I do not like to look back and say, "I wish I had done something". On this subject, I want every kid that was my friend in those days of early integration to know, I do wish we could go back in time so I could and would invite any friend to my neighborhood. If that friend had asked me, "Will I be ok?" I would respond the same way my friend, Jerome Nelloms, responded back then, "Folks will have to go through me to get to you and nobody is going through me."

The above is an example of how others have an effect on our decision-making process. Although I did not know it at the time, I was an outside the box thinker. I had the right intentions about what was right and what was wrong but I let other less open-minded people stunt my growth. It takes experiences to help people reach their full potential. It is important for people to learn from everything they have done, both right and wrong in their lives and we should never stop learning.

"We all go to work at 18 or 22."

Academics at Northside High were second to none and my High School Principal, Mr. Kelly, was a terrific mentor, as well as a great person. Mr. Kelly had a positive influence on every student.

I was sent on occasion, to the Principal's office only to have him sit down with me to explain that if I wanted to play football in college, I needed a high school diploma and a good high school recommendation. He treated all his students with respect and a great deal of discipline. I think about Mr. Kelly when disciplining my son, "How would Mr. Kelly handle this situation." Most of the decisions we make, as adults, are the result of what we were taught as kids.

In high school, the following recognitions helped me plan for a business career after high school and college. I was voted to the top 100 high school football backs in America, All State player in 1967 and 1968. I made All City and was the only white student that made both the WIGO and the WAOK black all-star teams. I was awarded the Gabe Talbert award as the MVP/best athlete in the city of Atlanta in 1968. I was also a member of the National Honor Society at Northside High School and maintained a solid B academic average. I did not become a professional athlete, thus the saying, "We all go to work at 18 or 22." Most of the best high school athletes never get paid a dime but they all go to work after high school or after college, as was my case as well.

Life's Lessons Learned From Playing Sports In High School

1. High School Sports are the best times in many of our lives and when most of us build our core values that we will live with the rest of our lives.
2. The unknown is scary but new healthy experiences make people better.
3. Personality will make or break most people. Have fun along the way.
4. Do not let closed minded people affect your individual ideas or thoughts.
5. Balance between athletics and academics are important throughout our entire life.
6. Ninety-nine percent of athletes never get paid a dime to play the game they love, but we all get paid to play the business game.

Chapter Four

Does that little boy play with those big men?

This chapter describes experiences playing football at the University of Georgia and an unsuccessful try to play pro football. Most people that play college football are B players and not the super star A players. We B players are given a limited amount of chances to show our ability. We must make good when given the chance. Often, the difference in an A player and a B player is perception. Those of us that do not look the part are given fewer opportunities to show our ability on the field in sports, business and life. This chapter shows examples of what we can do if we believe in ourselves and are not afraid to try.

Bob Blackwell was the best Pop Warner coach in America. Waymen Creel was the best High School coach in America. Now I am coached by Vince Dooley and Erk Russell, two of the truly great college coaches in America. How could any young man have better leadership?

The habits taught playing football for and being associated with Coaches Creel and Blackwell got me ready to go to the BIG LEAGUE, The Southeastern Conference. The fundamentals, attitude and discipline taught by Coaches Creel and Blackwell are the reasons I believed I could compete at the University of Georgia.

At age 17, at the end of my junior year at Northside High, I was offered a full scholarship to attend the University of Georgia. I quickly accepted and signed a letter of intent. My father and Coach Creel had attended the University of Georgia, so I was comfortable with my decision.

Coach Creel standing middle, Coach Russell standing left, Dad sitting

I was happy to take the burden of paying my college tuition off dad. At 5ft 8.5 inches tall, 185 lbs and not real fast in the forty-yard dash, Coach Dooley and Coach Russell were taking a chance. I am certain Coach Creel had a lot to do with the offer and would love to know the details of their conversations. I feel certain their conversation centered on things we can't measure.

The truth is Coach Dooley and Coach Russell coached the same fundamentals as Blackwell and Creel. Dooley was very organized, all business and coached a lot like Coach Blackwell. Some folks might question the comparison of a great college coach with a Pop Warner coach but the similarities were many. Both taught 100% team, both were very business driven. Both were tough, but fair and terrific men with no vices.

Coach Russell was a great motivator and coached in a similar way to Coach Creel. Russell and Creel always had a great game plan and to be in their presence gave all their football players confidence.

All of these coaches believed in working harder than anybody else. They sincerely loved their athletes and coached the TEAM concept. They all believed and through their example taught the "Yes I can" attitude. They were hands on and led by example. These men would never ask an athlete to do anything they would not do themselves. The trust we had for all these great coaches was due to their actions, not their talk. All people should be held accountable for what they do, not what they say.

One jump changed the coaches' perception

Prior to 1974, freshmen athletes were not eligible to play on the Georgia varsity football team so the first time I was noticed by the varsity coaches was in the spring of 1970 when I was a sophomore. Coach Gary Wyant, the defensive backfield coach, wanted to see our jumping ability. He asked us to jump and touch the goal post. I was the last player to jump. The highest leap prior to my jump was made by a 6ft 3-inch kid that got his forearm on the cross bar. This was an opportunity to shine. "Yes I can" jump and I put my elbow on the cross bar. It was about time for me to show something special. I don't think I had ever jumped that high. Adrenalin is a great asset. Being nicknamed "Super Frog" because of my leaping ability gave me the team feeling needed to gain confidence and better compete.

"Super Frog"

For the first time, I felt confident competing on the football field as a varsity athlete. Because I could jump high, folks began looking at me as a football player that might have some ability.

The difference in respect before I jumped and after I jumped was night and day. Having a coach start to teach me, gave me confidence I needed to believe in myself. The support of a coach can make the difference in winning and losing for any person in sports, business or life. All people in positions of leadership (sports or business) should try to center on giving strong support to all the people that are in the realm of their responsibility. If one's confidence level is high, look out for what one can do but if ones confidence level is low, do not expect good things to happen. The power of the mind (Attitude) does make the difference for any athlete's or business person's success or failure.

One play to sink or swim

The University of Georgia's 1969 defensive backfield was rated #1 in the SEC and all four players that started in that backfield were returning to play during the 1970 season, my sophomore year. Also, the coaches had already penciled in their 2 punt returners. These facts, coupled with the coaches mentality in the SEC during the early 70's not to start a sophomore at any position, made it almost impossible to break into the starting rotation as a defensive back or on the punt team. All of the top athletes in the 70's went to the big schools and Georgia had 140 players on scholarship that were sophomores, juniors, seniors or red shirts. There was a lot of competition. My worst nightmare was sitting on the bench. I knew that was not an option for me. I was not going to sit on the bench.

Coach Pyburn, the defensive linebacker coach at the time, was in charge of setting up and practicing some punt returns one day. I was on the sidelines watching the bigger, older, faster and better-built players getting all the attention as they were returning punts. I still had skinny legs and a little fat around my stomach. It reminded me of the first time I played for the Buckhead Red Devil Pop Warner football team. I was shy as a sophomore at Georgia but wanted an opportunity to show what I could do returning punts. Most importantly, I remembered what my Dad told me as a little boy playing touch football with the older kids in the neighborhood, "If you want something, you will have to ask for it." So, I opened my mouth and said to coach Pyburn, "Coach, will you let me run back a punt?" Coach replied," Do you think you can run back punts at this level?" I said, "I am only asking for one chance, coach." After a few more punt returns by the already penciled in punt players, Coach Pyburn pointed to me and yelled, "Get back there and show me what you can do." As I went back to get ready to return the punt, my high school "personality" broke loose and I said to Coach Pyburn, "This return is for you, coach."

I caught the punt clean and returned it all the way for a touchdown. As I ran back in excitement, I said to Coach Pyburn, "Do you think I can play at this level?" The rest is history. I probably never would have returned punts at Georgia if I didn't ask for the opportunity that day. I probably would have sat the bench my entire sophomore year and possibly longer.

After showing ability to catch punts effectively, the coaches decided to let me run back punts the first game of the year against Tulane. A sophomore returning punts in those days would be like a freshmen punt returner in today's world. Being a first year player coupled with the fact returning punts is one of the most difficult and athletic things in football, the coaches had good reason to be concerned. I helped erase their concerns by returning the first punt ever punted to me in a college football game 62 yards for a touchdown. I played free safety the entire year and intercepted 6 passes including 2 from Archie Manning of Ole Miss and ran back one more punt that year for a touchdown. I was a step slow in the 40-yard dash but fast enough on the football field. I was named to the All-SEC football team in 1970 and the Atlanta Journal/Constitution named me the defensive sophomore of the year in the SEC.

BUZY DISCOVERED BY ACCIDENT

Rosenberg Is an Attention-Getter

by JIM MINTER
Atlanta Journal Executive Sports Editor

ATHENS, Ga. — Georgia's coaching staff is using its Buzy Rosenberg time to applaud the Atlanta sophomore's Southeastern Conference leading punt return average rather than take credit for it.

"To be perfectly honest, we discovered Buzy by accident," admits Gary Wyant, the personable defensive backfield coach. "In the spring, we worked Bill Darby and Buck Swindle back there."

"Buzy first got our attention this fall in a pre-season scrimmage in Sanford Stadium. We had some injuries, so we stuck Buzy back there a couple or three times and suddenly he took one all the way.

"WE THOUGH it was a good thing he had done, but we still didn't realize he had this uncanny ability we know about now. So we went into the opening game with Tulane still considering Darby our punt return man. Well, you know what happened. Buzy zipped one back 62 yards for a touchdown and the job was his.

"I know Jake Scott was great," Wyant adds, "but this little guy is naturally one of the best I've ever seen. He has a tremendous ability to stay alive in traffic, which is something that comes natural and can't be taught."

To date, Rosenberg has hauled 19 punts back for 275 yards and a 14.4 average. He added an 80-yard touchdown return against Vanderbilt Saturday. It was reported as 78 yards in game reports, but films clearly show he made an extra two.

Rosenberg, an all-state halfback at Northside High in Atlanta, is reluctant to take all the credit.

"YOU HEAR talk about team efforts in football," he points out. "Well, a long punt return is one thing that's got to be a team effort. If you make it, you know somebody gave you some good blocking."

Wyant and Rosenberg agree a long punt return usually happens soon after the receiver gets the ball.

"I figure I've got to get away from somebody my first few steps," Rosenberg says.

"The punt return is a predetermined play we work on all week," Wyant explains. "I think a good one happens in the first 10 yards. We tell Buzy he has to be prepared to beat two people at the start, because very seldom do you see a perfect wall set up. When he does get into the wall, he gets some help and probably at the end he's got to beat one defender all by himself."

Surprisingly, Rosenberg isn't very fast. "We clocked him at a 4.9 40-yard dash in the spring," Wyant says. "But really, I think he runs faster. He does have an ability to turn the corner that 95 per cent don't have. His stride is deceptive and there's no question he has some fine moves."

In addition to returning punts, Rosenberg plays another important role for the Bulldogs.

"HE'S THE guy who keeps us loose," Wyant says. "He's not a comedian, but he's an athlete who has some ability and knows what to do with it. He always comes up with some comment you didn't expect to hear."

Unlike some college players who enjoyed stardom on offense in high school, Buzy says he honestly doesn't mind being a one-way defender.

"Returning punts is offense," he says. "I don't know of anything more enjoyable."

Wyant says Buzy, or Froggy, as his teammates call him, is ahead of schedule as a sophomore corner back. He got that job when Phil Sullivan was injured before the season. He got the Froggy tag because he jumps so high.

"I just think I'm lucky to be playing," Rosenberg says. "Georgia doesn't sign many little guys, and I'm just 5-9." He weighs 180.

"No," he says, "I never worried about being overlooked because of my size when I was in high school. Heck, I thought I was big until I got over here."

Staff Photo—Charles Bennett
Buzy Takes a Breather—80 Yards and a Touchdown Later

"Every Individual success is the Result of a Team effort"

I was nervous but not scared and because of the team's support, I was ready to play against Tulane. The following is my recollection of my first college punt return.

It was exciting to start at free safety and return punts at this level. I did not know what to expect. I did get comfort and support from Coach Dooley and Coach Russell. Once they committed to let me play as a sophomore, they did not look back. They were confident in my ability and they expected good things from me. Their confidence was what I needed. Because of the support of two great coaches and mentors, my confidence was high..

Named 'Sophomore of Year'

The ball was kicked and it was a low punt that I could not catch before it hit the ground (something I hated because the #1 job of any punt returner is to never let a punt hit the ground). I ran as fast as I could but the ball hit the ground before I could catch it and took a quick bounce up the field where I fielded it. My adrenalin was at its highest point. I moved 62 yards faster than I ever knew or thought I could and scored a TD. I do not remember my feet touching the ground and I know I moved the first 20 yards as fast as anybody has ever run 20 yards. The only time I can remember feeling like I did on that run was when I was chased by a Doberman Pincher through a neighbor's back yard at 11 years old. Adrenalin is a funny thing but it sure can make up for anything that one might lack other wise.

I ran back six punts for touchdowns while playing football at Georgia, two as a freshman and four as a member of the varsity team. I want to thank every member of our Georgia teams because when a person runs a punt back for a touchdown, you can bet he had a lot of help from his teammates.

My best day returning punts at the University of Georgia
"One day to remember being in the Zone"

Our first game of the 1971 season was played against Oregon State. It was a perfect day for football (72 degrees with beautiful blue skies). I told my dad, when I scored a touchdown, I would raise my hands to wave at him. Little did I know that day we would set several Georgia punt return records and one NCAA punt return record. We ended the day with 5 punt returns for a total of 202 yards and two touchdowns. I did raise my arms on both touchdowns to wave at Dad.

The day was like a dream come true for me. The first punt I fielded against Oregon State drove me backwards about 10 yards to the Georgia 20 yard line. I fielded the punt clean and had to make several moves to dodge the first two Oregon State players that were on me very quickly. After picking up some momentum I saw an open field but still had to figure a way to get through several defenders. I remember running all over the football field. When I saw the final opportunity to break for the score I hoped I had enough energy left, not to get caught. I was fortunate to find just enough speed to get into the end zone. It would have been upsetting to run approximately 150 yards and not score a TD.

Our second punt return for a TD was 66 yards and I had to make the best move of my life on this return to get free to score. I caught the ball and moved up field to my left and just when several Oregon State defenders were about to hit me, I did a spin move that I was surprised I had. Once I broke free from the crowd, I picked up a convoy of blockers to run with me the rest of the way.

We ran another punt back 37 yards and I think we could have scored another TD, if we had the same focus that we displayed earlier when we returned the first two punts. Our team could have been the only college football team in history to return three punts for touchdowns in one game.

When you think you are doing well, a little extra effort might make you do great. This is a terrific lesson to learn. I do thank God for giving us one day like the Oregon State game.

The Atlanta Journal sports writer, Furman Bisher, wrote the following article on the punt returns that day and this bit of writing by Mr. Bisher has meant a lot to me over the years.

"Don't Punt It, Mail It" ~Furman Bisher

The text of Dr. Thorington's sermon at Northwest Presbyterian church Sunday morning was taken from the 12th chapter of Romans and marked this trail of thought. "So we are to use our different gifts in accordance with the grace that God has given us."

Based on that commandment, Buzz Rosenberg should be playing tennis or golf. On the wrestling team, lifting weights, or president of the literary society. Surely, he should not be let loose to play center on the basketball team, or, as the case happens to be, delegated to prevent giants of men from catching football passes.

During a University of Georgia game last season, a fan rabid in the act of spectating, and his enthusiasm encouraged by his alcoholic intake, turned upon Leman Rosenberg Senior, Buzz's father and said, "If that kid was 2 inches taller, he'd be All-American and it's your damn fault!"

THE GEORGIA OREGON ST. SERIES

By Dan Magill

Georgia's two-game series with Oregon State ends with today's contest in Sanford Stadium.

Here's hoping the series finale has as many thrills as the first game provided September 11, 1971. Georgia fans will never forget the punt return performance that afternoon by Leman Loeb (Buzy) Rosenberg Jr. of Atlanta.

Little No. 34 (5-9, 175) electrified a crowd of 50,709 by going "all the way" 79 yards with the Beavers' first punt. It might have been the most brilliant run in the history of Sanford Stadium. Charley Trippi, among many others, thought so.

At first, however, Buzy's jaunt brought more moans than cheers because the turf was covered with several red objects misconstrued by fans as officials' flags. It turned out that the red objects were pieces of Buzy's uniform torn off his tearaway jersey by would-be Beaver tacklers.

Buzy was not content with that 79 yard gem. He returned four more punts of 37, 4, 66(TD) and 16 yards for a grand total of 202 yards — an average of 40.4 and a new NCAA record.

With Buzy setting the pace Georgia went on to beat the Beavers, 56-25.

Incidentally, ole Super Frog, as his teammates tabbed him, is back in Athens this fall as an assistant coach with the Georgia freshmen.

All-SEC safetyman Buz Rosenberg returned two punts for TDs vs. Oregon State (79 and 66 yards) in 1973. Here are three sequences of his 79-yard jaunt.

Rosenberg threads Oregon State defenders en route to a 79 yard punt return for a TD in Georgia's 56-25 win in 1971.

Since his birth 20 years ago, the Rosenberg off spring has gradually assumed the size and shape of his father, a clothing merchant and not a bad amateur golfer. These physical specifications work fine in the father's adventure, but at a height of 5ft 9 inches, the young Rosenberg frequently finds himself shuffling through a forest of belly buttons and hairy chests and offensive shoulders looking for a football that some quarterback has delivered in his direction, with full intent of taking advantage of his compact construction. Such is the plight of a defensive halfback.

If he were in horse racing, Rosenberg would be the jockey. If he were in ice hockey, he'd be the puck. If he were an automobile, he'd be the foreign car.

As is, he is in football and he turns out to be the tallest 5 ft 9 inch player most of us have ever known. As it turned out last year he wasn't all American but he was all Southeastern Conference. As it also turned out, defense, as considered in the normal vernacular, was not what he did best. Many a Georgia opponent reached the point that it preferred to mail the football back to the bulldogs rather than punt it. Rosenberg was just the sort of precocious imp who could turn the simple defensive process of the punt into six points for Georgia.

His style of returning a punt differs from the norm. He doesn't run it back. He's one of these rare fellows who transforms a punt return into the decathlon event, a combination of sprinting, broad jumping, hurdling, wrestling and steeple chase.

Somewhere along the line of his football career he has become convinced that the only legitimate way he should be stopped is by a court order.

There are just a few safety men in this country who have that "different gift" by which he can register with more impact on a college scoreboard than the offense. Dickie Harris of South Carolina is one of these, Tommy Casanova of Louisiana State, Joe Bullard of Tulane and Buzz Rosenberg of Georgia, all 5 feet 9 inches going on 5 feet 8 inches.

It was a warm, gluey Saturday afternoon in Athens. Sweat coated human bodies in a substance that felt like mucilage. The new Bulldog offense was, in three short series, beginning to resemble the Bulldog offense of 1970. The glamour backs hadn't yet shaken the stage fright and Andy Johnson, the sophomore quarterback, was showing a reluctance to call his own number.

Enough Film for GWTW

It was at this time of the opening game with Oregon State that the wee Rosenberg took matters upon himself. With a football in his hands, one player five feet nine is just as big as another player six feet four, if he applies that "different gift."

What Buzz Rosenberg does not have in one respect he made up in another. He was violently determined that he should make his way with a punted ball from Georgia's 21-yard line to Oregon State's end zone without interruption. And did.

Unfortunately, I find myself a little addled as I try to describe his course, I do recall three broken tackles. I do recall him leaving two large chunks of his shirt at the 30-yard line. I do recall him hurdling some Bulldog who tripped in front of him. And I do recall him spurting by the punter, a sophomore named McKenzie, and another Beaver into the end zone, totally exhausted.

In those old movies Hollywood used to make starring Ronald Reagan and John Derek as "The Gipper" or "Ol 98," that run would have required enough film to make "Gone With The Wind." The Gipper's whole life would have flashed back before him. He would have had his date book filled twice between the 50-yard line and the end zone.

Later Rosenberg ran one back 66 yards for another touchdown. And another 37 yards that set up another touchdown. Oregon State, on offense gained 89 yards by running the ball, Rosenberg 202 on defense.

I suppose you think now that that kind of exciting stuff is all Rosenberg does. He just gets to the field in time to put on his No. 34 and consents, after Vince Dooley pleads for a while, to run a few punts for touchdowns.

I'll have you know this kid is just another one of the hard working boys. He defends against passes just like any other kid on scholarship. In fact, he was defending against guys Saturday like the most appropriately named player on the field, Clark Hoss, who is six feet, eight inches tall and all "Hoss." Twice Rosenberg battled down two dangerous passes. Another he intercepted. Six times he tackled Beavers, or as many as any other Bulldog tackled.

I know you're going to wonder if anybody else played. Of course: in fact, everybody who could walk without crutches. Rosenberg only scored 12 points. The others scored 44.

The skills necessary to be a good punt returner	
• A passionate desire to return punts.	• Be tough minded and aggressive.
	• Have good instincts.
• Being able to run and catch at the same time.	• Have good quickness.
	• Fair catch the ball as a last resort.

"On any given day, any team can win"
 "Yes I (we) Can"

Georgia beat Auburn in 1970 at Jordan Hare Stadium. We were 28-point underdogs and they were ranked #2 in the nation with nine wins and no losses. Auburn beat Florida 68 to 0 two weeks earlier and had a bye week the week before playing us, while we were playing the same Florida team they had just beat. We lost to Florida 21 to 17.

Pat Sullivan, the future Heisman trophy winner, and Terry Beasely, one of the fastest and best receivers in the country, led a great Auburn team. This was the best football team I would ever play against. The truth is, nobody gave us a chance to win the

game. During the week's practices, Dooley and the coaching staff
were unusually serious and did the best coaching job getting us
ready to play one could ever imagine. We knew exactly what to
expect from Auburn but our ability to execute was the question.
This is the only football game that when I said my prayers before
going out on the field, I asked God to not let us get beat by more
than 3 touchdowns. Every football game I ever participated in prior
to this one, I always asked God to help us play our best and
hopefully our best will be good enough to win. When we went on
the field to warm up, something happened that we will never
forget.

The Auburn players were trying to intimidate us by pointing
fingers and laughing at us. All of the Georgia defensive backs
came together but did not say much. We all hated the lack of
respect. As Coach Dooley always said, "One for all and all for
one" would be the only way to beat this great Auburn team. To a
man, we might have been intimidated before we got on the field
but we were mad now and we wanted to fight. We wanted to get
on the field and G.A.T.A. My final prayer before the game was
"Please help us to play the best that we can and we will beat this
team." We went to the stadium thinking we might get blown away
but now our attitudes had changed. We beat Auburn 31 to 17 that
day in what many people consider one of the biggest upsets in
college football history.

To this day, the 1970 Auburn football team is the best team that
Auburn has ever had and the best football team that I ever played
against. We beat Auburn on that particular day but had we played
Auburn any other time, they would have beaten us by A LOT.

It took my teammates and I a few weeks to get over this victory.
We lost to a very average Georgia Tech team only one week later.
This is another lesson that sports teaches, do not rest on your past
wins, stay focused or you will lose soon.

The Georgia/Florida football game has always been a fun tradition. In the 70's and 80's the record was 15 wins for the bulldogs and 5 losses.

The first Georgia/Florida game I played with the big boys was 1970. We had control of this game and should have won but we lost. Florida had a good passing team with the duo of John Reeves throwing to Carlos Alvarez. We were winning late in the 3rd quarter by a score of 17 to 10 and driving for what would have been the winning TD. We ran the ball from the Florida 2 yard line to go ahead by a score of 24 to 10. Our running back actually got into the end zone but he forgot one thing, the football. The ball was fumbled into the Florida end zone and the Gators recovered. One play can make a big difference in a ball game, in business or in life.

The Gators had new life and we were deflated. We had the lead at 17 to 10 but we lost some confidence and Florida began throwing the ball on every play. The Gators began a drive early in the 4th quarter from their 20-yard line. Reeves threw a corner/ post pass to Alvarez and as he caught the ball, I put a big hit on him. Carlos did not get up but he did hold on to the ball. The Gators were now at midfield and driving. Carlos was sent to the sidelines for a few plays and the Gators kept driving. Carlos got back in the game and he caught the tying TD pass on that drive. The score was 17 to 17 with most of the 4th quarter left to play. The Gators went on to score again and beat us 24 to 17.

In 1971 we had one of the best Georgia teams of all times. We had 10 wins and 1 loss. We won the Georgia / Florida game by a score of 49 to 7. Every person on our team played well. Our defense was good and our offense was great. Everything went our way. We were upset from losing the year before. We were rated the #4 team in America after that win and we had a good shot to play Nebraska for the National Championship, had we won out.

The 1972 Georgia / Florida game was a most memorable and fun game. I got to play linebacker on some passing situations to cover Nat Moore of Miami Dolphin fame. Nat was an excellent running back at Florida before he became a very good receiver for the Miami Dolphins. I might have been the smallest linebacker ever to play in the SEC. Coaches Dooley and Russell were at it again and their plan worked great. We were up 13 to 10 late in the 4th quarter. Florida tried to hit Nat with a quick pass and I was in good position to make the interception. We won the game by a score of 13 to 10.

The Gator Bowl was always a good place to play football. We loved the short grass on the field, the great crowds and the warm weather. We all loved the bowl atmosphere. It was like another home game to us Dogs.

It is easier to stay on the first team in both sports and business if you are reliable and present.
"Yes I can"

Never missing a practice or a football game in a four-year career is probably my best accomplishment. I was hurt once. My injury happened while returning a punt in the 1st quarter of the 1971 Gator Bowl. I was pushing off the turf with my right foot when a North Carolina player tackled me by landing directly on my foot in such a way that the blow tore ligaments. It was a serious injury that would affect my ability during my senior year. I was not concerned about the future when it happened; I was concerned about staying in the game and beating the Tar Heels. Because of being in the heat of battle, I could run well enough to compete and ended up playing the entire game.

Prior to getting hurt, North Carolina's 5ft 10 inch and 215 lb running back (I think his name was Jolly) had run over me and I wanted to get him back before the game ended. This guy and I hit head on and he knocked me on my back and then stepped on my chest and went another 10 yards before being tackled. Sports are humbling and a good teacher for what is to come later in life.

We ended up winning the game by a score of 7 to 3. Coach Dooley beat his brother, Bill Dooley. Late in the game North Carolina was behind and had to score quickly. They began throwing the ball. They sent Jolly on a swing route up the sidelines and I read the play, as they threw the ball to Jolly, I put a good lick on him. When he was getting up, I said, "I've been waiting the whole game to get you back" he smiled. Always have fun and show personality along the way.

If I missed a practice, someone might be discovered, and this thought kept me focused. I would not be a small man sitting on the bench. This fear is the primary reason I did not miss a practice playing football at Georgia. Obviously, luck also came into play.

I did get knocked out cold one time at the University of Georgia. It happened during spring practice in 1971. Ricky Lake, a 210lb running back, always ran hard. Ricky was all muscle and during my entire football career, he ran the hardest and hurt the most to hit of any running back I ever hit. The Atlanta Journal/Constitution had named Ricky the Offensive Sophomore of the year in the SEC the previous year. I had learned, the harder we hit people, the less chance we have to get hurt. It always hurt when Ricky ran the ball. He ran a dive play and broke it for about 10 yards before we put a helmet-to-helmet hit on each other. To this day, all I remember is waking up on the sidelines stumbling around asking to get back in the scrimmage. The coaches did not let me play again that day. I had been knocked out cold for a few minutes. I never asked Ricky if the hit hurt him. To this day, I respect Ricky Lake as the toughest running back I ever hit.

"Does that little boy play with those big men?"
"Yes I can"

After one of our games at the University of Georgia, I saw my Grandfather and began my way over to see him when a little girl asked her father, "Does that little boy play with those big men?" She was talking about me. I turned to look behind me only to see the two tallest players on our team walking directly behind me. Craig Hertwig was 6 feet 9 inches tall and Barry Collier was 6 ft 7.5 inches tall. I really did look like a little boy amongst big men.

I was a little man playing in a big man's sport. I was small and a step slow, as well. How does a small man compete at a top level against people bigger and faster?

The mind is much more important than the body and adrenalin (competitiveness) is the hidden secret. This lesson was taught early by Waymen Creel and Bob Blackwell and reinforced by coaches Dooley and Russell.

The things we measure are not as important as the things we don't measure. We cannot measure competitive drive, common sense, work ethic, 100% effort, playing smart, coach-ability, TEAM centered, will to win, adrenalin, and attitude.

> *"It's a game of Attitude, pure and simple. It's not about ability: never has been, never will be. Everybody in this league has got ability."*
> *~Coach on the NFL*

The above quote applies to business or life.

> *"It is not the size of the man that makes a winner, it is the size of the heart in the man that makes a winner"*
> *~ Blackwell*

I did not look good on paper. My strengths as an athlete in those days were not measured. I was only 5ft 9 inches tall standing on my tiptoes (really about 5ft 8.5 inches tall). I played much taller because of being able to jump (never measured back in those days). I was 185 pounds or less but played heavier because of God given strength. The stronger the hands and body, the fewer missed tackles. I was a step slow in the 40-yard dash but much faster on the football field. Earlier in this book, on page 23, you have already seen the picture of the fastest kid in the city of Atlanta chasing me on a 70-yard touchdown run and I distanced myself from him on that run. This is a kid that could beat me in a 100-meter dash by 10 yards. Adrenalin and being able to use it effectively is mental and cannot be measured. The will to compete is a great motivator.

Good support from our coaches, teachers and mentors centers on the importance of things we cannot measure, taught early in life by Coach Waymen Creel. I am an example of a person with many physical deficiencies who worked hard to improve them and simply refused to listen to people telling me I can't.

The bottom line is people can do what they believe they can do in sports, business or life. The power of one's attitude is and always will be much more important than any physical deficiency or any negative opinions.

Always accept who you are because you cannot change what God gives you. Do not ever let any person tell you what you cannot do. Only the person inside the body has that right.

> *"On paper I was a 5 foot 8.5 inch, 185 pound Jewish boy but in my mind I was a 6ft 3 inch, 225 pound bad ass."*
>
> *~Attitude 101*

"Adversity shows a man's true character"

I don't remember much about the week I sat the bench at Georgia. I don't even remember what team we played. I do remember it was my senior year and a difficult week. I deserved to be put on the bench. I made a couple of dumb mental mistakes that I shouldn't have made. The coaches had no choice but to bench me in hopes of helping me get my focus back. I was at a cross road in my athletic life but sitting on the bench was not an option. The lessons learned throughout my life were solid. Quitting was not an option as well. Being able to accept responsibility and put the blame squarely on my shoulders was the reason I was able to fight back and regain the starting position quickly. All of us are knocked down many times in life, the question is, how fast will we get up and what will our attitude be when we get up? A person never losses in the long term unless he quits.

"It's not whether you get knocked down; it's whether you get up."

Hula Bowl

Playing in the Hula Bowl was an experience that opened my eyes to just how good the football athletes at Georgia were. The people who played with me in the Hula Bowl in 1973 were the best players of their era. All of the following players were in the NFL after graduation.

- Billy Joe Dupree – Michigan State tight end.
- John Rogers – Nebraska – Heisman trophy winner – flanker.
- Brad Van Pelt – Michigan State – line backer.
- Greg Pruett – Oklahoma – running back.
- Sam the Bam Cunningham – USC – fullback.
- Joe Ferguson – Arkansas – QB.
- Don Strock – Virginia Tech –QB.
- John Hannah – Alabama – offensive line.
- Charles Young – USC – tight end.

There were many good athletes participating in the Hula Bowl along with the above mentioned. It was fun being able to compare these All-Americans with the University of Georgia players. We had the same caliber of athletes playing football at Georgia. Jimmy Poulous was the best open field runner I ever tried to tackle. Andy Johnson was a pure athlete and second to none. Horace King, running back, Chip Wisdom, linebacker, Royce Smith, offensive guard and many others could have competed on the same field with the Hula Bowl players.

I had one interception and covered Johnny Rogers, the Heisman trophy winner from Nebraska, the entire game. My best memory was catching Mr. Rogers from behind at the end of the 1st half. We, the South Team, won the game. The lesson learned is sometimes we think others are better than we are because we believe what we read or because we do not know their weaknesses. We think people with other teams have something more than what people on our team have. The truth is, athletes are athletes, people are people and if a person is a good player on one team he or she will be a good player on any team. This is a lesson to be used in sports, business and life. Always believe in yourself.

I was actually put at 1st string defensive corner from the first time our Hula Bowl South team practiced. I suppose Coach Dooley and Coach Russell told Frank Broyels, our Hula Bowl coach to give me a shot. What an experience to play against the best to find out how you will fare.

The New Orleans Saints:
The end of an interesting football career

I was injured my junior year in the Gator Bowl while playing the final game of the year against North Carolina. I never fully recovered during my senior year. My freshman, sophomore and junior years were productive with good results. My senior year was not an indicator of what I could do at 100%. I was invited to play in the Hula Bowl and did have a good football game. I was getting healthy and beginning to think if given the opportunity, I could compete at the next level. The New Orleans Saints signed me as a free agent and told me they would look at me as a punt returner, safety and special team's player.

I wanted a fair shot to compete in the NFL to find out what the results would be. I was in good physical condition; the ligaments that were hurt in my foot were much better. I was looking forward to getting back to my old form shown during my sophomore and junior years.

I showed up in New Orleans mentally ready to overcome the fact I was not a physical looking guy. I had overcome the small person perception in sports all my life and wanted a chance to compete on the field to show my ability.

I was looking forward to the challenge of playing football until I met the New Orleans coaches. The New Orleans coaches were obviously not impressed with me. They were not respectful when meeting me and did not show any of the winning qualities my four hall of fame coaches taught. It was obvious that I was not going to get many looks. It reminded me of the first time I played with the bigger, older kids in my neighborhood. I thought about the Fritz Orr Camp experience. I remembered the Red Devils and I thought about my first game in high school. I also thought about what I had to do to win a spot on the University of Georgia football team.

In those situations, I had to overcome my physical appearance and needed to perform when given the chance. The coaching staff of the New Orleans Saints did not know my physical strength, my jumping ability, my competitive drive or my toughness. They simply looked at my size and in their minds I could not play in their league. It was embarrassing but overcoming other's perception was common practice for me. I was looking forward to putting on the pads and getting one chance to do something that would catch a coaches eye to change there opinion. I was mentally tough but did need an opportunity and at every level of life, once I got the shot, I proved that I could play.

The New Orleans Saints released me without giving me an opportunity to get on the field and compete. They simply called me in the office and said you cannot play for us. I got on a plane and flew home. The Saints in those days were the worst football organization in the NFL as far as victories go. Do you think the poor winning habits practiced by this organization might be the reason why?

I was ready to move into another chapter of life. Football was over. A business career with National Distributing Company was in my future. I was blessed to have the great experiences and meet the great folks I have talked about in this book simply because I was a football player.

The New Orleans Saints experience at the end of the day is a better result for me than if I had made that team. I learned what it felt like to be discriminated against, to not be given a chance because of what I looked like. If given the chance and supported, people will often surprise you with their ability that otherwise would not have been noticed.

Life's Lessons Learned Through the Influence of Sport in College

1. Winning habits and winning attitudes take a lot of repetition before they become a part of any person's daily personality.
2. A nickname is a good thing.
3. Confidence makes the difference in winning or losing.
4. Always learn from your mistakes.
5. Sometimes you need to aggressively ask for the opportunity to be successful.
6. One's will to win or competitive spirit can overcome most obstacles.
7. "B" players can have "A" days.
8. When you think you are doing well, a little extra effort might make you do great.
9. Mental toughness will help one overachieve and accomplish a lot.
10. High energy or Adrenalin can make the difference in winning or losing in sports, business and life.
11. Making a positive out of a negative is centered on one's attitude.
12. Support people and give everyone a chance to succeed or fail.
13. Do not rest on your past wins, stay focused or you will lose soon.
14. It is easier to stay on the 1st team in both sports and business if you are reliable and present.
15. What a great experience to compete against the best to find out how you will fare.

Chapter Five

Academics in College

The truth is the athletic dorms at most universities have as high an academic average as regular college dorms. The education and tutors offered to college athletes is the best. If every college student that failed out of school were recognized the same way athletes are recognized when they fail school, the papers would be filled with college dropouts. This chapter shows examples of the strong education athletes receive in college.

The education one receives is the responsibility of the student because people will receive exactly what they put into their education. Most Universities have strong programs to offer. Students that graduate from college should be prepared to start their business careers.

People, who do not take advantage of what their University has to offer, will regret the lack of effort later in life. Education and sports take work ethic, discipline and a competitive attitude to reach one's full potential. College offers an opportunity to learn that all students should take advantage of and be thankful for.

The Real Estate degree received at Georgia has returned big dividends throughout my life. Real Estate has been a strong second income for many years. Lessons learned in college made investments in Real Estate much easier.

The General Business degree received at Georgia has been a great help to me in the corporate world. I have met and talked to people from all walks of life that have received educations from many top schools. The education received at Georgia can compete with any of them.

It was encouraging to read that the University of Georgia was rated among the nation's best universities by U.S. News & World Report. In fact, UGA was ranked #58 ahead of such schools as Ohio State, Boston University, UConn, Clemson and Indiana University. The School of Business was ranked #27, ahead of such schools as Georgia Tech, Tulane and Colorado. The Real Estate Department at the Terry School of Business (named after two great Jacksonville Dawgs, Herman and Mary Virginia Terry) was ranked # 5 nationally.

Our coaches pushed academics and when a player needed assistance, tutors were there for us. I never saw anything like the allegations recently made against former UGA Basketball Coach Jim Harrick in which his son, who also was made a "Professor", created a course that became the laughing stock of college athletics. While I attended UGA, any athlete, regardless of their ability and talent, had to go to class and his classroom performance was reported to the coaches.

I also recall the Jan Kemp days at UGA, which fortunately occurred after my tenure, in which UGA was accused of "favorable" treatment of athletes. I wasn't there so I can't really comment, except to say that Coach Dooley was and is one of the most honorable men I have ever known and would have never bent the rules in order to win football games.

Review the Football Letterman's Club 2005 directory. This directory list the past football lettermen at the University of Georgia. It is interesting to recognize the number of ex-football players that have gone on to become successful business people. The transition from football to business can be an advantage if an athlete takes the lessons learned playing football and applies them to business practices.

The number of vice presidents, executives, business owners, lawyers and doctors has never surprised me. If a person has the discipline to play four or five years of college football and graduate, he has already accomplished a lot in life. The lessons learned on the football field coupled with getting a great education is a strong formula for success. It was an honor to play in the same defensive backfield at Georgia with the following people.

Dick Conn is the owner of Carolina Campus Supply. Buck Swindell has a company that manufactures sportswear. Jerome Jackson owns Consulting & Training Principle, the James Paul Group. All of these teammates received a good education at Georgia. They were taught by good coaching and good teachers and have transitioned these lessons learned into rewarding business careers.

The number of successful football athletes from Georgia is an endorsement of the great education the University of Georgia gives its athletes. The education received at Georgia is as good as any and the above proves that those who studied at Georgia graduated with good potential.

Life's Lessons Learned

1. Balance between sports and education is important.
2. One will get back from school exactly what one puts into learning.
3. Most accredited colleges have a good curriculum to learn from. The responsibility to learn is the students.

Chapter Six

Once a competitor, always a competitor
The "Character" of sports last a lifetime

Athletic competitions after college are fun and beneficial to anyone's overall success. Experience helps people compete and win. "Yes I can" beats "No I can't" every time. Focus and a "Will to compete" make the difference. Combining sports with business after college makes any person better at both.

Most jocks in high school or college are jocks for life. We were led by our coaches in our youth, but must find the way by ourselves as we age. It is not easy to transition from playing competitive sports through our youth and then all of a sudden, the games are over. The facts are we get better physically until our late 20's and can maintain athletic excellence into our 30's, 40's and even 50's.

Physical fitness is important to continue as we age. The balance between business and physical competition is important just as the balance between academics and athletics were important in school. The fun most of us have as we age is through competitive sports. Golf, bowling, bicycling, running, ping-pong, etc. are all fun throughout our lives. Do not let others tell you "You Can't."

Without a doubt, sports brings out the best in people. If we had more business managers using the winning habits learned from sports, our business environment in America would be much better.

The transition from a sports environment to a business environment happens at sometime in every athlete's life. This transition is difficult for some and a natural evolution for others. Some folks find it hard to be the star athlete one day and just another fellow the next. The key to having an easy transition is how balanced you have been prior to leaving athletics or what your attitude is when you leave organized sport.

If your friends are from a wide variety of back grounds, if you have balanced academics and sports, if you have worked on a social education, if you have been humble and recognize every person has different strengths and different weaknesses, the transition will come easy and be a natural evolution into your next adventure or challenge in life. If you go into business with respect to all, practice the winning habits learned through playing sports, are willing to learn and want to be successful, sports will play out as a great benefit that will open doors that otherwise would not be opened. However, if the athlete goes into business and has an attitude that he is owed extra attention or with a cocky personality, people will turn on you in a hurry. The bottom line is an athlete has a big advantage if he uses what he learned playing sports to make him successful in business and life. People that have not played sports in most cases have not been exposed to the leadership and discipline most athletes have been exposed to.

The following are some of the athletic competitions I continued to pursue after school. These competitions coupled with working in business kept a good balance and taught me a lot. It is fun to test your will to win, your competitive attitude, your discipline, how you challenge yourself and how character built early in life works to help you win later in life, in sports and business.

Winning when others think you can't is the ultimate fun. The following physical fitness competitions were important at the time.

We all have memories and lessons learned to talk about and I encourage you to never quit competing.   Always follow your dreams no matter how old you are. We build character competing in sports our entire life. Do not let others tell you "you can't." Even hard core Rappers learn from team sports

> *"This film is about how I learned to be a good father through coaching."*
> ~Snoop Dog on his upcoming movie
> Coach Snoop

Competition in our 20's is easy to find.

At 25 years old, winning the American Fitness City of Atlanta sit up competition and pull up competition was fun. Losing the dip competition was humbling. The sit up competition consisted of doing as many inclined sit-ups as you could in one minute. The incline bar was set at the steepest level possible. The number to beat was 72 sit–ups in the one-minute limit. Most people in the gym thought 72 would win this competition. To the surprise of most, I did 78 sit–ups in one minute that day. I have never tried again. The ability to focus and the mental attitude to win learned at a young age gave me an advantage. Winning the competition was not as important as challenging myself to try. Making a 100% effort was important. People learn every time they are challenged in sports, business and life.

The reason for writing this chapter and talking about post college athletic competitions is to show what can be done and what can be learned by continued athletic competitions and having the right attitude. Competing to keep a young and healthy competitive spirit works wonders for anybody's attitude.

The dip competition did not have a 60 second time limit. I did 74 dips, a personal best. Some guy did 98 Dips. It was impressive to watch. Winning is trying and giving a 100% effort. Losing is not trying or not giving a 100% effort. Challenging yourself and giving your best is uplifting. The lesson learned is to appreciate your competition's ability and talent.

Winning the pull up competition is a good example of how discipline always wins. I had done pull ups every day for years. The technique developed over the years was better than anyone else. The discipline learned early in our lives last forever.

Playground Basketball

Playing basketball at Hammond Gym in Atlanta with the best athletes in the city was a good outlet for the competition we all needed. We had strong basketball competition and the local talent was excellent. It would be interesting to know how some of our teams would have competed against the TV playground legends of today. On occasion, there would be 10 athletes, 2 or 3 under 6ft tall, on the court playing basketball and every person could dunk. Atlanta Falcon football players would bring a team of 4 or 5 people to compete with the local talent. We loved to play against the Falcon football players. We usually beat these high paid athletes. They came in the gym cocky and left the gym humble. We do have many good athletes in this country that have never been paid a dime. The combination of strong athletic competition along with going to work every day is an advantage and necessary for those of us who love to compete.

Always Challenge Yourself

At 28 years old, it was a fun challenge to bench-press over 400 pounds and then 5 minutes later run a mile in less than five minutes. It dawned on me that I had never heard of another person doing such a thing. The body type of most people that run a mile under five minutes is the opposite of the body type that can bench press over 400 pounds. When people have physical challenges, their attitudes are better at work and play. It took several months.

It was time to compete and do this self-imposed challenge. Accomplishing this goal was special and to this day has been a strong motivator for me to go after any challenge put in front of me. Everyone should dream up challenges for themselves. It's great fun and helps people keep a positive attitude.

The Most Physical Man in Jacksonville

— Staff
Buzz Rosenberg never doubted that he would win Confetti's Most Physical Male contest.

Winning the most physical man in Jacksonville competition was rewarding. Committing to compete was the result of another person telling me I did not have the ability to compete.

While listening to the radio, I heard that Jacksonville was going to have a contest to find Jacksonville's most physical man. It got my attention. The initial weekly event consisted of 30 minutes of grueling calisthenics (push ups, running in place, sit ups, grass drills etc) followed by a very difficult obstacle course that ended with a 40 foot rope climb. The competition was geared towards a combination of strength and quickness events. I ran the thought to enter this contest by my General Manager at NDC. He said, "You are too old to compete and you will embarrass yourself." The discussion reminded me of the two guys that told my dad I would never be big enough to play football for the University of Georgia. I immediately called the radio station to enter the next week's competition. Don't ever let someone else tell you what you cannot do. The only one that has that right is the person inside the body.

The competition lasted 10 weeks with a winner every week and then a final competition at the end to find the champion. I won the third show. My work was not finished. The grand finale was to come and there were some good competitors to beat. The final night was a lot of fun. Competing as the underdog is a big motivator for most of us. Being the oldest person in the competition, I was picked to finish in the middle of the pack. The final competition consisted of 30 minutes of aerobic exercises i.e. running in place, deep knee bends, vertical jumps, stretching, leg lifts, 30 grass drills and 30 slow push ups followed by the difficult obstacle course.

The obstacle course consisted of running through a series of tires, then crab walking back. Then, we did 10 one-arm push ups with each arm and crawled through a tube. We had to jump 20 times with a heavy rope filled with water, followed by scaling a wall 12 feet high. We then slipped into inversion boots to hang upside down on a bar and do ten inverted sit-ups. Then, while wearing the heavy inversion boots, we had to do 15 pull-ups. After that, it was over the wall again. We then put a spoon in our mouth and had to carry an egg 20 ft and drop it in a bowl (balance was necessary). The final challenge was to climb a 40-foot rope and ring a bell.

The driving force was to tell my General Manager I had won this physical competition. His negative comments were the motivation needed. It was fun placing the winner's money on his desk the next morning. He was surprised but happy and told me he would never tell anyone what they couldn't do again. We both laughed and have been friends to this day.

Winning the "Most Physical Man" in Jacksonville competition at 34 years old is an example of what experience and mental strength can accomplish. Simply believe you can, have no fear and give it your best shot. The results can be surprising. It is fun to do things others think you can't.

Old Dogs vs. Young Dogs Alumni Football Games

The 1983 and 1988 Old Dogs vs. Young Dogs alumni football games were very physical competitions. Playing in two alumni football games in the 80's brought back memories that motivated all of us. Meeting and seeing the people that had played in the 70"s and the 80's was a great time. Some of the older players came to win or at a minimum knock the young dogs around a good bit while others came for the social gathering. We all loved the competition. One thing will always be certain, once a competitor always a competitor.

We had some good alumni players returning to play in these games. We thought our offense would have a tough time scoring because the offense needs to play together for a good bit of time before it jells. We did think the young dogs would have some difficulty scoring on our alumni defense and we were right on both thoughts.

Dooley at the 2nd alumni game in 1988

It was great meeting some of Georgia's best players. Because of our mutual Georgia football background, we all had football experiences that made us respect, love and appreciate each other.

It was fun playing in both alumni games and teaming up, once again, with Jerome Jackson, Dick Conn and Buck Swindle in the defensive backfield. All four of us played together in college and became friends for life.

Jerome was very smart and tough. He is one of the best safeties to ever play for Georgia. Dick Conn and I played on the same Pop Warner team together at 12 years old, the same college team together and now the same alumni team.

Dick was a very good defensive back with terrific work ethics and a fearless, competitive attitude. He went on to play pro-football with the great Pittsburgh Steelers and has a Super Bowl ring to show for it. Buck played at 6ft 4 inches tall and was a great athlete that would be just as good in today's world, they all were competitive and looked good in both G day games.

1987 20-year Post Integration State of Georgia All State Team – A High School Honor

20-year all-state team

The 20-year all-state team

Pos.	Player, School	Grad.	Comment
OFFENSE			
QB	Buck Belue, Valdosta	1978	accounted for 6,700 yards and 87 TDs
RB	Herschel Walker, Johnson Co.	1980	Rushed for 3,167 yards as senior
RB	William Andrews, Thomasville	1975	Led team to two AAAA state titles
RB	George Rogers, Duluth	1977	Back of year as junior with 2,300 yards
WR	Danny Buggs, Avondale	1970	All-American in high school and college
TE	Stan Rome, Valdosta	1974	Holds national receiving mark with 4,477 yards
OL	Joel Parrish, Coffee	1973	"Cowboy" later led Georgia to SEC title
OL	Lee North, Shamrock	1978	Two-time all-SEC at Tennessee
OL	Bill Mayo, Dalton	1981	Two-time all-state and AAA lineman of year
OL	John Davis, Gilmer	1983	Later became "the refrigerator mover"
OL	Winford Hood, Therrell	1980	Two-time AAAA all-state selection
K	Kevin Butler, Redan	1981	Two-time All-American at Georgia
P	Ray Guy, Thomson	1969	Perhaps the NFL's best all-time punter
DEFENSE			
DL	Freddie Gilbert, Griffin	1980	The best pass rusher in state history?
DL	Jimmy Payne, Cedar Shoals	1978	Later an All-American at Georgia
DL	Ronald Simmons, Warner Robins	1977	Led Demons to 1976 national title
DL	Larry Kinnebrew, East Rome	1978	Remember "Big Brew's Wrecking Crew"?
LB	Mackel Harris, Americus	1976	Led team to 13 shutouts in 1975
LB	Lucius Sanford, W. Fulton	1974	Four-year starter and All-American at Tech
LB	Ben Zambiasi, Mt. de Sales	1974	Leading tackler for '73 state champs
LB	Chip Banks, Laney	1978	Two-time AAAA all-state selection
DB	Scott Woerner, Jonesboro	1977	Defensive star of Georgia's national champs
DB	Jim Bob Harris, Clarke Central	1978	Led team to AAAA state title as Sr.
DB	Buz Rosenburg, Northside	1969	Two-time All-SEC at Georgia

Being picked in 1987 to be on the 20-year Georgia All-State football team that consisted of the best 11 offensive football players and the best 11 defensive football players to play in Georgia from integration in 1967 until 1987, was a big honor.

Some other players of recognition that made this 20-year All State Team are:

- Buck Belue at QB – Buck nosed out Andy Johnson because of the job he did playing at Valdosta High. Buck later led the University of Georgia to a National Championship in 1981.
- Herschel Walker – Heisman Trophy Winner.
- George Rogers – Heisman Trophy Winner.
- William Andrews – great running back for the Atlanta Falcons for years.
- Stan Rome – held the National Receiving mark of 4,477 yards.
- Joel Parrish – later led Georgia to the SEC Title.
- Lee North – 2 time All-SEC at Tennessee.
- Danny Buggs – All-American in high school and college.
- Ray Guy – All-Pro and the best punter of all time.
- Kevin Butler – Still kicking in the NFL.
- Scott Warner – All American at Georgia and a great punt returner. Scott and I received the postgraduate Hall of Fame award together.
- Ben Zambiasi – a terrific line backer at Georgia and then in the Canadian football league.
- Jimmy Payne – an All-American at Georgia.
- Freddie Gilbert – one of the best pass rushers ever.
- Lucious Sanford – All-American at Georgia Tech.
- Ronald Simmons – a great middle guard for FSU and a great pro wrestler as well later on in life.
- Larry Kinnebrew – "Big Brew the Wrecking Crew".

To be placed on the same team with the above athletes was an honor that I will always cherish. The older we get, the more we appreciate the people and the experiences playing sports gave us.

The American Gladiators TV Show
~Getting picked as one of four people out of over
1200 applicants who tried out for the show was
much more difficult than actually doing the show.~

While standing in line, I noticed a young man looking in awe at the bigger, stronger athletes that were determined to win a spot on the local Orlando show. I could see there were many strong athletes ready to compete. Over the years, I had learned that looks do not matter and if you let a man's appearance intimidate you, you probably have already lost any competition.

After listening to the young man talk about the athletes that were getting ready to compete, I asked him, "Do I intimidate you?" He looked at me as if I was crazy and then smiled and said "No." I replied, "If I don't intimidate you, nobody should intimidate you because I am going to win this competition today." He then became interested in talking to me, "Why do you think you will win?" he asked. I said, "I have competed all my life against bigger, better built, faster athletes. I have learned through experience to never be intimidated by anybody and to focus on what you can control, not what you can't contol. Attitude, preparation, and will to compete will determine the winner today." I suggested he quit wasting energy worrying about people that were not going to win. We sat down to relax and wait for the competition to start.

The competition consisted of doing 50 finger tip push ups in a minute, running the forty yard dash in under 4.8 seconds, doing an obstacle course and then doing 18 behind the neck pull ups in one minute. People were omitted for any of the above that were not completed. Only 18 people completed this faze of the competition. While standing around waiting for the final events to begin, the 21 year old I had talked to in line tapped me on the back to tell me he had made the finals. It was good to see him in the finals.

The tough man events were yet to come and they consisted of one competition similar to a one on one tackling drill in football. This competition pitted two people against each other with one carrying a volley ball (offensive person) who had to dunk it in a cylinder by dodging the defensive person whose job was to tackle the runner or hit the runner as hard as he desired to keep the runner from accomplishing the dunk. Each contestant played both the running position and the defensive position. The judges wanted to see if we were physical and tough. We wore leather helmets, a mouthpiece and competed on a mat. At 2 months short of 42 years old, playing a one-on-one tackling drill for the last time was a dream come true for me. My competitor was a 6 feet, 1 inch, 210 pound, well built 25 year old. He was a cocky kid. He took a look at me and seemed happy he got me as his competitor. Most of the final competitors were younger, stronger, and bigger than me.

Don't judge a book by its cover was about to be taught again. He tried to run directly through me without even making a head fake. The element of surprise does work. I hit this kid with everything I had. He had entered into an element of competition he was not ready for. I learned in high school that I would rather make a big hit than make a long run. After the hit, I motioned for him to do it again but he decided the one hit was enough and quit on me. My football lessons from the past paid big dividends on that day. I loved the competition. The young man I was pitted against could have competed at a high level had he been taught at an early age how to win. He was a physical kid but once he knew he was in for a war, he quit. The lesson re-enforced here is, "Yes I can" beats "No I can't" every time and "a quitter never wins."

Four athletes competed at the Orlando arena and it was a good competition Emceed by Mike Addemly. One of the competitors was a 28-year-old man that had won the Florida triple jump State Championship and also was a 100-meter state finalist in high school. In the obstacle course, the final event of the American Gladiator competition, he had a three second head start. It took everything I had ever learned, plus a lot of adrenalin to win the show. It was a major upset for me to beat that young man in the final event. All of my great coaches were with me the whole way.

The "Yes I can" and "never quit" attitude came through at the end. Winning, when others think you can't, is the ultimate fun.

The Gladiator show went on to 68 different cities in the USA in 1991. After all the shows were complete, the producers picked 28 athletes from over 30,000 competitors to compete on the TV show held in Hollywood, California. I got the phone call, inviting me to come to California several months after winning the show in Orlando. I suppose I should say the producers picked 27 kids and one old man.

Left to Right: Shawn Hargrove, Buzy and Ernest Peace

Our time in California was fun and the contestants nicknamed me Pop. The next oldest contestant was 32 years old. Every athlete picked to compete on the TV show in Hollywood California in 1992 had to earn their way. There were thousands of good athletes that did not even make the original competition in their respective city. The most impressive thing was to see the speed and strength these kids exhibited. Many of these competitors could have played football in college or even the pros. Never have I seen so many good athletes in one place.

The better the competition, the more fun winning becomes. The TV show that pitted Earnest Peace and Shawn Hargrove against myself was probably the most physical gladiator show ever produced. It was their speed vs my strength and it was 41 years of learning how to win vs. young men that probably were not as determined to win but were probably better athletes. The "Be a Winner" lessons taught and drilled into my head through the influence of four great football coaches made me a winner in California.

The experience of participating on the American Gladiator show re-enforced that older people can compete at a high level in sports. It also re-enforced that there are many top athletes who are not professionals. Don't let age hold you back. Have fun along the way.

"If you can't beat them physically, beat them mentally."

The Georgia Tech alumni football players challenged the Georgia Bulldog alumni to a flag football game in 1995. I was 45 years old, in good physical condition, and had maintained some pretty good quickness. Although I had retired from playing flag football at 40 years old because of continuously pulling leg muscles, I figured this would be a good opportunity to see some good friends, bring back some good memories and maybe get a few plays in.

It was a game played for charity and held at Bobby Dodd Stadium in Atlanta. It was fun but anytime the Bulldogs and the Jackets get together, the competitive juices begin to flow. We had SEC football officials call the game. To stand there and look across the field at the yellow and black made us all know that the game was on and there would be no prisoners. I knew the Tech players felt the same when they saw the black and red of the Bulldogs. We both wanted to win. The team rosters were filled with mostly younger players in their 20's and 30's so the older players did not plan on getting much playing time.

To make matters more difficult, it was a cold winter day. Cold weather is not what the older guys wanted or needed to get loose. I played split end. We had not scored and it was late in the 1st quarter when I got into the game.

On the first play in the game, it was important to size up the ability and attitude of the defensive back responsible for covering me. Experience is a big advantage in sports, business and life. Seeking to understand others before we try to be understood is one of the seven habits of highly effective people that works in sports and business.

The defensive back covering me looked to be in his early 20's and he gave me exactly what I was looking for. He lined up on top of me and said, "Old man you can't beat me, I'll be everywhere you go all day" and then laughed with his other defensive friends. I laughed with him and said, "You're right, I just want a few plays and then I'm getting off this field." The lesson, "Do not ever judge a book by its cover" was just about to be taught again.

There was no question in my mind, because of the cocky attitude of my competitor, we would beat this kid deep on the next play. In the huddle, I asked our Georgia quarterback to throw me a streak route. He said he was going to put the ball up no matter if I was open or not. As we walked up to get into position, I looked over at my young competitor and smiled as I said, "This is my last play, son. I'm getting off the field." He was laughing and not focused on defending the play. We did score by completing a 60-yard pass. I ran faster than I could run. The kid was in shock and embarrassed. He learned a lesson for life. Always respect your competition and never pre judge anyone. It was fun competing with the young athletes of the 90's. Many of the football players of the 70's era would compete just fine with the kids in the 90's.

Competing in many athletic competitions in my 20's, 30's, 40's and 50's has taught me success is always the result of good leadership and the "You can" instead of "You can't" attitude. This attitude coupled with experience, gives any person the winning edge in sports, business and life.

"Physical Fitness is an asset in Business and Life."

Most folks do not believe a person can do 100 push-ups or 50 pull-ups in a minute. These two body weight exercises are great physical fitness tools for all of us. Push-ups and Pull-ups are exercises that anybody can do at any age. I challenge any person reading this to call me when you get to 90 push ups in a minute or 50 pull ups in a minute. It takes desire, patience and discipline.

At 14 years old, in a PE class at Northside High, we had a push-up competition to see who the strongest kids were. I got beat by an 8th grader named Bubba Cooper. Bubba is a great guy and a good friend but I did not like losing to him that day. If you do not like losing, do something about it. The next day after losing to Bubba, I began doing push ups every day. I got up to doing sets of 60 push-ups every morning and every night. I have never lost a push-up competition since Bubba beat me.

After losing the push up competition, I started doing pull-ups every day as well. I did pull-ups every night on a pull up bar placed on my door to my bedroom. Pull-ups are more difficult to perform than push-ups. If the coaches decided to have a pull-up competition, I did not want to lose. To accomplish one's full potential, all physical exercises must be done with the best technique. Technique will be improved considerably through years of practice. My personal challenge is to be able to win pull-up competitions at 60 years old. Only time will tell.

"To be the best you have to beat the best"

Tony "the Gladiator" Conyers is an employee of NDC who competes at a world-class level in weight lifting. While on a trip in the Bahamas with several of my NDC teammates, we all were waiting on our flight to get back to the states when one of the guys challenged the rest of us to a push up competition. All ten of the young folks were eager to compete and jumped at the chance to show how many push ups they could do. The winner did 50 push ups and was very proud of himself. I was challenged to show what I could do. My football personality broke loose and I responded, "If I am going to do as many push-ups as I can do, find me someone that can beat me." One of the guys mentioned "Tony the Gladiator." He told me, Tony was a world record holder in the 165 lb weight division for the squat and dead lift. He also said Tony could bench-press 451 pounds. "This is a man I would like to compete against" I replied. He laughed at me and so did every one of the other NDC reps. By laughing at me, they were saying I couldn't beat Tony, so don't even try. Again, no person has a right to tell anyone what they cannot do. Only the person inside the body has that right.

The next day after returning to Jacksonville, I couldn't wait to contact Tony the Gladiator in Tampa. I told Tony that his brothers in Tampa were bragging on him and laughing at me when I said he would be the type of person that I would like to compete against. Tony, being a great competitor, responded with respect by saying,

"I would love to compete with you." I am sure Tony has done many things during his athletic career that others told him he could never do. NDC was having a company picnic just a few weeks later, so I asked Tony if he would like to compete with me doing maximum push ups in a minute, maximum pull ups in a minute and repping 225 pounds on the bench press. He accepted my challenge immediately and laughed as he told me, "No 50 year old man can beat me." I laughed and agreed with him, but at the same time told him "The competition is what we both feed off of." The match had been set. Tony was responsible for bringing the bench press and weights. The park had a tree limb we used as a pull up bar and we could do push ups anywhere.

I was excited and called all the guys that told me about Tony to let them know we had set up a match to compete with each other at the annual company picnic. They laughed and thought I was kidding.

The day of the picnic came and to everyone's surprise, I showed up to compete. Tony was a well-built man that stood around 5 feet 6 inches tall and looked to weigh a solid 165 pounds. Tony was a pleasure to meet and we both looked forward to competing.

When it was time to compete, we did push ups first, pull ups second and the bench press last. I have always been confident in my push up and pull up ability and did not know for sure but thought I would beat him in the bench press competition as well.

Push-ups in a 1-minute time span was our first exercise and Tony went first. Tony did 65 push-ups in the minute. I did 66 push ups and stopped at 66 because I wanted to conserve energy and strength. Every NDC employee was surprised at the push-up competition.

Pull-ups were next and Tony went first again. Tony got 32 pull-ups in a minute. I did 33 pull ups and stopped because the bench press competition was next. The score after two events was pretty much a shock to everyone watching, except my girl friend and me.

Going second was an advantage for me because knowing the number to beat meant I would not have to max out on push-ups or pull-ups. Being able to save some energy for the bench press competition was a good plan.

The bench press competition was last. Tony went first again and got 19 repetitions. I was not surprised that Tony only did 19 repetitions because the push-ups and pull-ups took a lot of his energy and effort. It was my turn to bench press and I felt good but when I got to number 16, my right shoulder gave out on me and a muscle tore. I was forced to stop and Tony won this event. Tony is a fun guy with a great personality. He whispered in my ear that he was sorry I was hurt but he was glad he won the event. Both Tony and I had great fun competing against each other. It is important for competitors to continue competing all their lives.

People thought I was as strong as Tony. I wasn't nearly as strong as Tony. Tony did a lot more weight on the bench press than I could do. He also could lift more weight than I could on the squat or the dead lift. Tony was competing with me in exercises that I have been doing all my life and all the other NDC people fell for it. If Tony had picked his strength exercises, I would not have had a chance to win. The perception at the end of these competitions was I was stronger than Tony. It is funny how folks think. Perception in sport and business is not always reality; another good lesson learned through the influence of sport.

Last fitness challenge.

On April 7, 2003, a complete hip replacement was necessary. I had limped around for three years waiting as my hip got worse until I finally had no choice. It was another challenge but through the influence of sport, it became a fun challenge. It was a game type situation. Setting goals had been learned early in life so I set several goals in relation to getting back on my feet after the operation. Most people were telling me it would take months of therapy or rehab. My goal was to be walking, driving a car and back to being independent within 6 weeks after the operation. The right attitude worked again. It has been two years since this operation and I want to tell anyone that has to get this type of operation, the results are great. Don't wait to get it done, waiting only gives your body wear and tear that might cause damage to other parts. This operation should have been much earlier.

The things learned later in life from the sports we played.

Most people have used the saying "If only I knew then what I know now." I hope at least a few young people read and listen to what most of us learn playing sports early in life, but do not fully understand until later in life. I was 40 years old before I fully understood the following facts that if a young athlete becomes aware of while playing sports, doors will open for him or her that will help them forever:

- As a good athlete, the fans love and adore you. Doctors, lawyers, farmers, house keepers, laborers, rich people, poor people, all people are pulling for you and for that time when they are watching you play your sport, you are the hero. Human Nature dictates that every human being wants to get back the same respect they give out. If an athlete in today's world is polite, respectful and gives back to the fans what the fans give to him, the sky is the limit. An athlete has a short span of time to be at the top of his game and this is the best opportunity to show your true character. Go out of your way to give tremendous respect to your fans.

- Always give 100% and if you think you can do something special, go for it. Most people look back on their careers and often get upset with themselves for not reaching their full potential. We wish we had worked on our weaknesses to make them strengths or at a minimum improve them. I ask every young person to look in the mirror and be honest with what you are weakest at and work at 100% to turn that weakness into strength.

- Appreciate what God has given you. The percent of people playing college ball is very low. Do not take your scholarship for granted. A college degree is very important in today's world. Work to learn everything you can in college because it will give you a head start in business.

- Watch your good coaches carefully and learn from their actions. Good coaches have winning habits and attitudes that if learned, will last a lifetime.

- Realize the friends you make in college will be more meaningful the older you get and you cannot have too many people talking good about you later in life.

- Enjoy every day you are in school, do not sweat the small stuff and at that age most stuff is small stuff.

Life's Lessons Learned from the
Influence of Sport as an Adult

1) Do not stop doing what you love to do.
2) You can compete in and learn from athletic competitions all your life.
3) Do not let opportunities to excel in sports or business pass you buy.
4) Focus, Attitude, Confidence, Concentration and Spirit can get better with age.
5) It is fun to do the unthinkable.
6) Always set goals.

Chapter Seven

Corporate Reality: Where is the Coach?
"Once you win a man's heart, he will follow you anywhere."

The character built through playing sports gives the athlete an advantage in business. The athletes that stay in bounds and learn the good habits taught by our coaches are often winners in business. This chapter shows real life examples of how the lessons and habits learned playing sports influence our winning character in business.

At 23 years of age, after receiving a degree in Real Estate from the University of Georgia and completing one year of graduate studies, I began my business career in Life Insurance sales with a major Life Insurance Company in Atlanta. I was offered the job because of my football career (an excellent example of how doors are opened in business through participating in sports).

I lasted 2 years, did an O.K. job but did not learn much. I was surrounded by people who had their own agendas and who had no time or interest in mentoring. I was only 23 years old and though I was eager to learn, I was very inexperienced. The truth is, they could have had a productive employee, but did not have a good mentoring program in place.

At 25 years of age I left the insurance business to begin what has become a rewarding career with National Distributing Company, an Atlanta distributor of distilled spirits.

I was hired in 1976 as a sales representative. My starting salary was $12,000 and my first account was 30 miles from home. I was responsible for auto expenses, including gas. I joked with NDC management that I was paying for the privilege to work for them. Working with NDC in 1976 is a good example of loving a job vs. working for money. If one has patience and loves what they do, success will come. Recognizing my limitations as a sales person, I immediately sought a mentor/coach/teacher.

Thank God for Football

After four years, I got my first promotion to become a District Manager. I supervised five people and had it not been for the leadership skills learned from participating in sports, I would not have known how to manage people

I ran our sales team using the same values that were taught throughout my athletic career. I was not a natural leader but learned leadership skills because, during my athletic career, I had been led by great leaders. "The key is to bring the average of your team to a high level," (Coach Blackwell's Philosophy) was my goal. Motivating through positive re-enforcement really does work. It is contagious for the entire team to talk about the 100%, "Yes I can" effort needed to be successful. Teaching the fundamentals of our business, operating with mutual respect, treating people the way you want to be treated, clearly communicating with others and teaching the importance of integrity to sales teams always creates winning results. Developing trust throughout any group guarantees success. Sadly, some of my peer's careers ended because they were never exposed to these values.

Another challenge

In 1982, I was asked to move to Florida to become the Sales Manager of the NDC wine sales team in Jacksonville. I never expected to leave Atlanta but after visiting Jacksonville and falling in love with the water and beaches, I looked forward to another challenge and accepted the position

This was a considerable move from a District Manager's position in that my new responsibilities would be setting sales agendas, tracking goals, inventory control, purchasing, supplier meetings, programming our monthly special sales deals, etc. but most importantly, supervising (Coaching, Teaching and Mentoring) three managers.

I had not been told that NDC was not considered the preferred supplier of Wine and Spirits in the Jacksonville market. Nor was I told that most of the NDC sales reps and NDC sales managers in Jacksonville were poor at customer service. I knew my work was cut out for me but in truth it was no different than when my dad took me in his car at 12 years old to try and make the Buckhead Red Devil football team. Sometimes not knowing is better.

"Work hard and give 100% and you are a winner", was my every day quote that Waymen Creel drove into all of his Northside High players. The first 3 years (1982-1985), work was all day every day 7 days per week. The winning habit of a good work ethic learned playing football gets any of us ready to do whatever it takes to win in business.

> *"We win together and we lose together"* – *Blackwell*

The Team Concept was at the center of my thinking. The basic leadership and character skills taught from sports during youth would play a major role in my success or failure. The irony of this new challenge and position was that it was easy to be a winner at whatever was put in front of me in business. I had learned the basic leadership skills necessary to win by four great leaders. In my 30's which were the 1980's, my business career flourished as I helped turn a bad team into a strong company by being a leader that influenced others to develop winning habits. At that point in my life, this was basic good business 101. My athletic experiences taught the importance of being at the front of the battle leading BY EXAMPLE.

The 1990's were good years for most businesses and for NDC as well. It has been fun sharing winning lessons learned from mentors growing up playing football. I have tried to improve the business culture in the corporate world wherever I could. Today, I am a Senior Vice President working for a good company and traveling the state of Florida sharing the same basic character building skills taught on the football field as a kid.

"It is better to try and lose than to not try."

In 2002, NDC created a new position, Senior Vice President to lead the State of Florida's off premise Wine and Spirits Division. The following is a very interesting scenario. Our President and I were not aligned with each other. My first thought was, do I want to work closer with the NDC President and am I willing to commit 100% to do what it takes to be successful in this new position?

We did have a capable person in the Jacksonville NDC office who was eager to move into my VP position. He did deserve to move up and was ready for the challenge. If I didn't go after this position, it would not be fair to him. I also received several nice phone calls from people I would be leading. They asked me to put my name in the hat because they wanted to work with me. The support of people who would be working with me was encouraging and appreciated.

I needed to analyze the new position as to exactly what the job qualifications would demand. I also needed to commit at a 100% effort to put whatever time it would take into this job to assure success.

After several weeks of thinking and analyzing, I committed myself at 100%. There were four strong competitors and I was the last person to throw my name in the hat. I did a lot of soul searching prior to committing and do suggest that if any opportunity to move up the ladder ever comes about in any business for any person, due diligence be exercised prior to seeking the new position. Do not ever take a position to satisfy your ego. Make sure any move within any company is something you really want to do.

"If a man does his best, what else is there?"

I was the underdog, but the truth is, sitting on the bench has never been an option and will never be an option. Getting picked to lead the off premise business in the state of Florida over three qualified people by a man that did not particularly like me and that did not understand me would be a major upset. To be the best, you have to beat the best.

This experience was similar to my sophomore year at Georgia when all of the defensive back-field positions had been penciled in with other player's names. The coaches did not realize sitting on the bench was not an option then and the president at NDC would soon come to realize sitting on the bench would not be an option now.

NDC created this position to lead the off premise wine and spirits business in the state of Florida in late 2002. I was told the decision had been made on the person NDC wanted for this job and it would not be in my best interest to go after it. Don't tell me I can't because only I have that right. This negative comment made me more determined than ever to put together the best presentation possible. If I were not picked, for whatever the reason, I would have given a 100% effort as my five father figures taught me during my youth. Our company policy is to post all job opportunities and anyone can apply for any open position. NDC would listen to my presentation.

I am a person centered on leadership and have never been a politician. Our NDC President and I had several disagreements over the years. I did not think I had much of a chance to land this new position but I had been taught it is better to try and lose than to not try.

"The man makes the position, the position never makes the man." ~ Creel

Preparation = Confidence = Winning

I put a tremendous effort into my presentation. At the end of the day, I was centered on making the best presentation possible and if I was not picked for the job, in my mind I gave it my best shot. I had fully committed to get this job and I wanted it badly. I had prepared well and made my presentation with confidence. Low and behold, after all was said and done, the company President chose me.

Maybe I was wrong about our state President. After all, sports teaches us that the true character of any person is what they do not what they say. It was exciting to get the job. I was ready for a new challenge. It is my goal to influence as many folks as possible with the same business habits learned from four great football coaches

"Well done is better than well said."

Life's Lessons Learned

1) If one has patience and loves what they do, success will come.

2) A manager's success should be directly related to the number of people he has influenced in a positive way.

3) New challenges happen in business every day and accepting these challenges with the "Yes I can" attitude creates winners.

4) Attitude and leadership skills necessary to win in sports become more important in business management the higher up the corporate ladder one goes.

Chapter Eight

Sports Influence on Business Habits

Why are the winning habits we learn playing sports often not used when it comes to business? The higher up the ladder a person goes, leadership skills become more important. Over time, people develop an opinion of a manager's leadership. At the end of the day, we all are judged.

You will read a few quotes in this chapter from people I have mentored. These quotes have been placed because when all is said and done, what people say about you tells a story. The compliments given to me are a direct result of doing my best to stay within bounds and to follow in the footsteps of my mentors. Recognize these quotes as being examples of what happens to any person that leads with the winning habits taught by playing team sports.

Mentors / Coaches / Teachers / Managers

The Dictionary defines a mentor, as "a friend entrusted with ones education" TRUST is the #1 trait of a mentor. The dictionary defines a coach as "one who instructs or trains a performer or a TEAM of performers", a teacher as "one whose occupation is to instruct," and a business manager as "one who directs, a boss."

Mentor – Coach – Teacher can be used as one and are synonymous. The definition of a manager is one of the big problems in business today. If it were synonymous with a coach, teacher or mentor, we would have better leaders and less point and click people in management positions.

Coach your sales reps the same way you coach your athletes. Most managers in business today spend too much time bossing and directing (point and click direction vs. in the street direction) and not enough time teaching, coaching, mentoring and leading. Sometimes a person's ego gets in the way. Management should be centered on leadership. The higher up the ladder one goes in business or sports, the better leadership skills one needs.

"The first time you meet Buzy, you can't help but notice his infectious good attitude towards life. Buzy has mentored me most of my professional career in the wine business. Although there are plenty of examples of good coaching I can write about, the most important example he has set for me is his definition of competitiveness. Being competitive does not mean beating the person next to you, it means being the best person you can be and build a good team around you by coaching your people to be the best they can be."

Jeff Statti, VP, Director of Wine Sales, National Distributing Co.

Buzy Rosenberg

"Super Frog" Now a Super Salesman

by Mike Cheatham

Ask the old cornerback/punt returner par excellence just which one of the recent Bulldog defenders he most admires, and his ready reply will not surprise Georgia loyalists.

"The little guy ... what's his name, Tim Wansley?" Rosenberg feels the parallels are evident, "I was a short guy, too in my career."

Rosenberg is proud to know that the 5-9 Wansley overcame a broken leg in his final game last season and after being a seventh-round NFL draft pick, made the Tampa Bay Buccaneers team this year.

Rosenberg lettered in 1970-1972 and made All-Southeastern Conference in two campaigns and even making preseason All-America.

And what was the colorful nickname of Rosenberg, the Atlanta Northside High product?

"Super Frog," admits the creation of Northside Coach Wayman Creel. Why, pray tell, one asks the Bulldogs' legendary Coach Vince Dooley? "Because no one ever leapt so high to defend an opponent in the secondary." Or, to hear others tell it, few others took modest-appearing talents to such great advantage in a career with the Red & Black.

Rosenberg comments on how he has had a lot of fun being Super Frog, even sending UGA publicist Dan Magill and others greeting cards emblazoned with a picturesque cartoon version of the frog character that teammates said he resembled. With the card went the player's profound thanks for "everything" they had done to advance his career with Dooley's "Dogs."

Columnist Furman Bisher once said, at 5-9, 175 pounds Rosenberg would have been more likely a candidate for the tennis or golf teams — or a captain of a school debate team. But it fell to Dooley's secondary coach in those days—former West Virginia quarterback Freddie Wyant — to give the most persuasive explanation of Rosenberg's natural talents, like returning five Oregon State punts for an unprecedented Georgia-record-setting 205 yard and two scores (career totals: 88 punts returned for 946 yards). In accomplishing that Buzy broke the long-held record by Lamar ("Racehorse") Davis in the Rose Bowl season of 1942. Wyant and defensive coordinator Erk Russell both conceded

"Super Frog" did not have blinding speed but stressed that his ability to break tackles and pick out clear lanes in returning the ball helped him achieve his success.

Bulldog all-timer Charley Trippi, too, marveled over those talents, adding "when Rosenberg sees daylight, he goes up the middle with it and he does a lot on his own." Trippi, who was perhaps the perpetrator of

Rosenberg threaded Oregon State defenders en route to a 79-yard punt return for a TD in Georgia's 56-25 win in 1971.

the Bulldogs' most spectacular punt returns, added, "Jake Scott was outstanding, but this kid keeps going when people are all over him — he has a tremendous instinct to see daylight."

Rosenberg's pyrotechnics on the field of play in his three-year varsity career definitely paid dividends. The Bulldogs moved up from 5-5-0 and a loss to Georgia Tech in 1970 to a spectacular 11-1-0 and a Gator Bowl win over North Carolina the following season. Rosenberg's valedictory came to a fitting close with a 7-4-0 chart in 1973.

Erk Russell claims the coaching staff knew what to expect when they recruited Buzy.

"He knew how to win coming from a program under Coach Creel, and he had good working habits," said Russell. "Even today, Rosenberg stands in awe of the coaching icon and attributes major portions of his success to Creel.

Those lessons learned at the feet of Dooley, Russell, Creel and others have stood him in good stead in the game of life. "Super Frog" is now a "super salesman" with National Distributing in Jacksonville — a liquor and wine wholesaler — and a renowned physical fitness buff, having appeared on such television shows as "American Gladiator." His mother, Barbara Rosenberg, now probably is somewhat relieved, as conditions have changed somewhat since she was quoted saying, "I just don't like to see all those big boys hitting Buzy — he's so little!"

Okay, Mom, but as an article produced by the athletic association on the old punt returner and defender flatly stated once, "He's still one of the mightiest little mites ever to thrill a Georgia football crowd."

If you ever saw him break to daylight in the open field, you're sure to agree.

The following are quotations from my football mentors that could and should be used in business communication.

1) Dooley – "one for all and all for one."
2) Dooley – "3 or 4 plays will determine the outcome of our success or failure today."
3) Russell – "do not ever ASSUME anything or it will make an ASS out of U and ME."
4) Russell – "if they don't score, they can't beat you."
5) Creel – "if you try at a 100% effort, you are a winner, the outcome of the game is secondary."
6) Creel – "Trust and integrity will build a strong TEAM."
7) Creel – "the man makes the position, the position never makes the man."
8) Creel – "The things we measure are not as important as the things we do not measure."
9) Blackwell – "The goal is to bring the average of your team to a high level."
10) Blackwell – "it is not the size of the man that makes a winner, it is the size of the heart in the man that makes a winner."

All four great coaches taught the same habits it takes to succeed in any venture (sports, life or business).

The winning habits taught by Bob Blackwell were the same ones taught by Coach Creel, Coach Dooley and Coach Russell. All of these coaches were great leaders and every kid taught by any one of these coaches should be a strong leader as an adult.

Dear Buz,

I hope all is going well in Jacksonville. Things are starting to settle a bit here with my new position in Pensacola and I was just reflecting on my career. You have had such an impact on my career and I thought I'd write a note of appreciation. It seems like our racquetball days were only yesterday and you obtained an interview for me with NDC. Little did I know then what a great career that day would lead to. You have always been there for advice, mentoring me along the way, and have played a pivotal role in shaping me into the professional I have become. I just wanted to let you know how much your guidance and genuine concern for my well-being is appreciated. I will continue to strive toward future success with NDC and will always remember your part in the opportunities I have been afforded here.

Thank you for not only being there for me professionally but also being a close friend for so many years.

I'll see you during visits to Jacksonville, and know that we're only a phone call away.

Sincerely,
Bryan Smith,
VP, Director of Wines,
Pensacola, FL

The most important practice for any manager is the ability to lead by being centered on teaching, coaching and mentoring. Sam Walton, the founder of Wal-Mart, and George Jenkins, the founder of Publix Super Markets are good examples of what strong leaders can accomplish when they are centered on teaching, coaching and mentoring. It is easy to point and click. It takes an effort to be seen and lead.

Is mentorship a lost art in the corporate world?

We want the best for our children. We want them to reach their full potential. Parents look for the best mentors, coaches and teachers. They want their children to have access to the most current technology available to obtain the best results. We want our kids to develop winning habits to be successful and happy in life. We want them to have things better and easier than we did. We love our kids.

Why don't the same parents that want the best for our kids put more emphasis on coaching, teaching and mentoring our employees who work within the realm of our responsibility?

1) Are we insecure?
2) Do we have a self-centered ego?
3) Do we know how to lead?
4) Do we understand the return on our investment of time to mentor others?
5) Do we understand our responsibility to coach and train our people?
6) Do we want our employees to reach their full potential?
7) Do we want our employees to develop trust in their company?
8) Do we want our employees to develop winning habits?

If you do not mentor others within your area of expertise, ask yourself why. A business manager will be measured by the people that he or she has coached upward. Do you want to be a business manager that has coached people up or a business manager who leaves a bad legacy?

Businesses must become more centered on rewarding their management teams for teaching their people the ropes of the game. Sharing best practices in the corporate world today is only a saying because it seldom occurs.

The more I talk to people about this omission, the more I realize the reason companies fail is they simply do not have systems in place to make sure their talented people reach their full potential. At the end of the day, a company is simply a team of people. The better any team of people work together, the more games they will win.

Good leaders are the most important asset for any company, athletic team or group. The sooner the corporate world recognizes its environment to breed followers vs. leaders, the better America will be and the more successful corporations will become.

> *"Having the ability to lead is not enough.*
> *The leader must have a passion to lead."*

All managers influence every person within the realm of their responsibility, either in a positive or negative way. Then their careers end and what have they contributed? Coaching people upward is vitally important. Consider these thoughts:

- Do you want people to miss you or be glad you're gone?
- Do you want people to say good or bad things about your business ability?
- Do you want folks to say good things about your integrity and honesty?
- Do you want to be remembered as a team player?
- Do you want to be remembered as a person who gave respect to your fellow employees, your competition and your personal friends and family?
- Do you want people to say, "He or she was a strong communicator?"
- Do you want to be remembered as a person who shared what you knew with others and cared about the success of others?
- Do you want people to have a smile on their face when they talk about you?

The real question is:

Do you want to be remembered as
an "I" person or a "we" person?

<u>Team 101</u>

"Trust"
"We" NOT "I"
"Us" NOT "Me"
"Ours" NOT "Mine"
"Secure" NOT "Insecure"
"Humble" NOT "Egotistical"
"Sharing" NOT "Self Centered"

Common sense says, "I will kill we" every time.
Every Individual Success is the Result of a Team Effort

"I have worked with Leman "Buzy" Rosenberg for the past 15 years. Buzy has been a great friend and a mentor to me over the years. His ability to coach and lead has been an inspiration to me, and his natural ability to be able to "relate" to people at all levels help me hone my skills on how to communicate with others.

Buzy's greatest influence on me, however, was not to let ego or emotions get in the way of making decisions in business, and ultimately to have balance in everything you do. That balance related to a much happier me, and being a better business executive."

Deborah Alfaro, Vice-President
Director of Florida Wine,
National Distributing Co.

Business Mentors

In 30 years of corporate business reality, two people have taken the time and effort to help me succeed and grow. When I met Bob Moore, he was 40 and I was 32. Bob was a District Manager with Publix Super Markets and he lived in Gainesville, Florida. The irony of our friendship was that we loved sports, loved business, and thought a lot alike, but Bob was a Bull-Gator football fan and of course I was a big Georgia boy. We actually made this difference a positive. In the 1980's I never said a word to Bob when Georgia won the annual Florida-Georgia Football game. Then in the 90's when Florida won most of these games, Bob never said a word to me. We are true friends that do understand each other.

Bob Moore is a dynamic business person and leader with great character that he says was partially learned through sports. He is the man most responsible for the terrific growth that Publix Super Markets has shown in Georgia, Alabama and Tennessee over the past 14 years. The fact that Bob is eight years older than me and has a lot of experiences to share has helped make it easier for me to get through my business career. Bob has always made me feel comfortable and his passion to teach and coach will never be forgotten. Bob is the Division VP for Publix in Atlanta today. The company is very lucky to have a man like Bob Moore as one of their executives.

As a 32-year-old upstart sales manager, I would travel a minimum once a month to see and talk to Bob. I used to tell Bob I needed my fix. The feed back from Bob actually reinforced the winning habits learned as a kid while playing football. He was always there for me and he is always there for me today as well. Lucky for many others and myself, Mr. Moore has a passion to mentor and teach others the character built from sports.

My other business mentor has been a friend since 1982 when I moved to Jacksonville. Bob Robison and I liked each other the first time we met and to this day are good friends. Bob was the director of merchandising for Publix Super Markets in Jacksonville, Florida. When I met Bob, he was approximately 46 years old. To this day, he will not tell me his age. I would guess Bob is a young looking 68 years old or so. Bob is a very successful man and retired four or five years ago. Bob and I have lunch a minimum one time per month to talk about everything and share our thoughts with each other. He is and always will be a good person for me to bounce my business plan off. Bob also believes the winning habits he learned playing team sports as a kid are priceless.

Both my business mentors are Publix Super Market employees and both are sports centered people. As I have learned, the Publix Super Market model was born by George Jenkins and centered on their people sharing, teaching and mentoring each other. Publix is the best-run super market chain in America. You think their "people centered" philosophy might be the reason? I do!

"Healthy" Competition is the ultimate "HIGH"

Competition is "The thrill of victory." Competition is "The agony of defeat." Think back about the last time you were really feeling good about something you did. I'll bet it had to do with some type of competition.

Most folks love either playing or watching sports. It makes no difference if the sport is football, basketball, baseball, track, ping-pong, pool, golf, or etc. We all are happy or depending on how competitive one is, unhappy after competing or watching and pulling for our favorite player or team to win. It is a natural high.

Most folks love to make a sale in business, put together a good presentation, be complemented for a job well done and be appreciated for the hard work they do every day. We all are happy when any business competition ends with a positive result and creates that natural high.

Competition occurs every day in our lives in one form or another. We all are human beings and the bottom line is to compete at a 100% level. So, if we win or lose we feel good about our effort. This is healthy competition. We may fool others about the effort we give but we can never fool ourselves about any effort that we have made.

Keeping a competitive spirit "healthy" is the bottom line to enjoying good competition. It is not healthy to compete over petty things or to make your competitor your enemy. Sports teaches us to respect our competitors and to play hard to earn their respect. Competition must be fun for it to be healthy on a long-term basis.

The great thing about the business world is if you want to challenge yourself, there are always a ton of challenges to overcome. You must realize you will win some and lose some and the bottom line is to give your best at all times.

Beware of the Spin Artist

A spin artist, generally speaking, cannot take criticism and is not centered on the truth. I have met and had meetings with many spin artists in my career. These people always go on the offensive when they should look at the reality at hand. They try to spin the facts to help themselves look better in any situation. A spin artist, in most cases, never had the leadership or coaching to understand that spinning is not necessary and that reality is always the best answer in the long run. Every person has weaknesses and people that look in the mirror to discover their real weaknesses can make these weaknesses their strengths. Spin artists never look in the mirror, because they are insecure and simply cannot handle the fact they have weaknesses. Being a big enough person to accept the fact you might have weaknesses is tough for a lot of people. Every person that has been successful in any sports competition has had a coach that tells him or her on numerous occasions what they must work on to be the best. Spinning is not an option.

People in business can learn from successful people in sports that success is REAL and will only be a false perception for a very short period of time. A spin artist cannot win in the long term and if we can get businesses engaged in a reality vs. unreal perception, a spin artist will not win short term as well. The best way to rid our environment of the spinner is to not accept this type of conduct.

"Make your dreams come true"

We all have good ideas or thoughts that we wish we had acted on. Learn from your mistakes. Having success in my 20's and 30's competing in athletic competitions and the corporate business world gave me the insight of the importance to act on any pro active thought or idea. I learned that knowing what the results would be even if they were not good is better than not trying and never knowing.

When I was in my late 20's and even early 30's, I thought about challenging the winner of the Super Star television show to a winner take all competition. The Super Star show was a gathering of professional athletes to compete in many different athletic events. The events they competed in were events I excelled at. Some of the challenges were weight lifting, 800 meter run, tennis, golf shot, pull ups, etc. The final event was an obstacle course. My dream was to challenge the winner of this television competition by putting up my own money to a winner take all prize. I should have tried to contact the show to issue the challenge. One never knows, a common person competing with top professional athletes might have been the first reality TV show. "If you have a talent or an idea that you believe you can excel at, give it your best shot now because it will be too late soon".

Being sucessful in real estate, winning the American Gladiator competition at 41 years old, winning the Most Physical Man in

Jacksonville competition at 34 years old, and winning the National Distributing Company state position as a Senior Vice President at 51 years old are all the results of following through with dreams. I am hopeful these are good examples for others to learn from.

> *"Every athletic or business accomplishment*
> *is the result of a TEAM effort."*
> *Dooley – "one for all and all for one"*

The reality is that any goal or accomplishment any person achieves is the result of a team effort. It takes the knowledge, the confidence others have in us and the strength received from the energy of others supporting and pulling for us to win at anything (business or sport).

> *"At 38 through 47 somebody's got to be there for you. I really thought about coach Knight and Tom Butters. There's a reason why somebody's in a place they are all the time. Those two people have been unbelievable for my development. If I didn't touch them in my life, I would not have touched so many others. I realize that."*
>
> *Coach Mike Krzyzewski,*
> *Duke basketball coach on*
> *winning his 700th game*

Knowledge – every athlete or business person had to learn his or her skills from a coach or mentor. Every Olympic champion has the best teachers and the best technology to draw from to be a winner, a complete TEAM effort. Every successful business person learns their skills the same way any athlete learns their skills. Knowledge to be the best comes from learning through others (Evolution).

Confidence- People must have other supporters to give them confidence to take on challenges and be successful. We need others to believe in us and team members who live and die with our successes or failures. We need to be continuously motivated and encouraged. Our mentors and supporters sometimes have more confidence in what we can do than we have in what we can do. Thank God for mentors or the team we have behind us telling us "YES YOU CAN."

> *"Yes, we are going to whup him." "Hearing my father say that inspired me. I had my dad in my corner and I won my first fight. Although I was the one in the ring, I won as part of a team."*
> *The Soul of A Butterfly*
> *Muhammad Ali*

Preparation equals Confidence equals Success

Preparation is working harder and smarter than your competition. The #1 reason that a team wins more than it loses is because of preparation. The confidence we had playing football for Blackwell, Creel, Russell and Dooley was in part because of the preparation of the game plan followed every week.

Personal success in business is easier after one learns the importance of preparation. Spend more time preparing for business meetings than anyone else. People prepared the best have more confidence. People with confidence will win.

Instinct can make the difference in winning or losing *"Yes I can"*

A person with good instinct is lucky. The difficulty is for any person to realize if he or she has good instinct. Instinct is meeting a person and within a few minutes being able to feel this person's positive or negative energy. I met two young men in their early

40's recently. Both of these young men looked good in their suits and it would seem they would have similar personalities. They had similar job titles and worked for big companies. They were both in charge of the meetings we had. One of these leaders allowed his second in command to lead the meeting and he stated he wanted to learn and listen. The other controlled his meeting and did not want any input from others.

One of these men was secure and sharing. The other was insecure and egotistical. It only took a few minutes of conversation to know who was secure and who was insecure. Instinct is an incredible tool that cannot be measured but is important in business. You have to be able to feel instinct. It is not measurable.

The more experience people have, the better their instincts become. Focus on making your instinct work for you. Instinct can be your best asset if you can learn to feel it.

The things we measure are less important than the things we do not measure in business too.

"Not everything that can be counted counts and not everything that counts can be counted."
~Albert Einstein

In the business and everyday world many things can be measured. We can measure the increase or decrease of revenue, the increase or decrease of Gross Profit percent (GP %), whether goals have been met and we can also measure aptitude.

We cannot measure common sense, work ethic, or productivity as it relates to personality at work or sports. We also cannot measure what one had to do extra to accomplish the goal (some goals are easier to make than others). A person's competitiveness, creativity, adrenalin rush, or instinct cannot be measured.

We cannot measure a person's ability to place people in the right position, if a person is clearly communicating, if a person has motivational ability, if a person can lead by example, is centered on trust and integrity, has listening skills, is a long term thinker, and if a person understands mutual respect.

Most big businesses are centered on what they can measure in black and white vs. what they cannot measure. The things we do measure will always be measured and at the end of the day, are very important. Businesses will get better results when the culture of big business changes. The pendulum will change in the future because for any business to be successful in today's changing times, things that are not currently measured will become more and more important.

> *"It has become appallingly clear that our technology has surpassed our humanity"*
> *Albert Einstein 1879-1955*

Setting Goals

"The most important of all goals is to reach one's full potential."

Some people set unattainable goals and then become disappointed when they do not accomplish them. Why set yourself up for failure? Why set a goal to be an All American football player before setting a goal to start on a college team? Why set a goal to be a vice president in business before setting a goal to be a first level manager? Why not set realistic goals? Set attainable goals you can achieve within a given time span if you work hard. Then set another higher goal with the same attitude. Make goals attainable and fun. Goals that are not attainable will hurt you more than they will help you.

"Computers are perfect, people are not"

The first time this statement was used was in 1996 at one of our weekly management meetings. We all were doing our best to learn word, excel and how to e-mail communication when it dawned on me that "computers are perfect and people are not." I didn't profess to know everything that was going to change drastically and quickly in the future, but I did begin to understand people must embrace the computer and begin to work every day on getting better at what they did or within a few years, business would leave them behind.

I remember speaking at the management meeting and telling our management team every person must begin learning the best way to use a computer to keep organized, because in the near future, computers would be used to measure everything that they did and "computers are perfect, people are not." The bottom line message was business will not stay status quo, it will change more in the next few years than it changed in the previous 20 years.

The main thought was to motivate every NDC manager to realize they must improve their skills. In the not so distant future, simply keeping the skill level they have now will not cut it. It was my responsibility to motivate good employees today to make sure they would be good employees tomorrow.

I also explained to our managers that they needed to be balanced with how they use a computer in the future. Good employees in the business world will suffer if their companies are not computer balanced. I felt that some management styles would use the information technology to find people doing things wrong more than finding people doing things right.

I did not know it then but today my prediction has become appallingly correct. Computers track and measure everything imaginable. It is important that people use the information at their fingertips with a sense of reality. No employee is perfect so be careful not to de motivate by using a perfect computer to find only the things that are wrong. I suggest that using a computer is great but realize that we must compliment more than we find issues. I also suggest that the things we measure are important but do not forget the things we do not measure are more important.

All managers must be seen in the market place. Only by getting out into the market can a manager learn the conditions, customer's attitudes towards your company, sales person's work ethic, and attitudes of the sales reps in the field. If all is well, make sure to compliment the employees on these most important fundamentals that are not measurable. We must not forget the reality in our business was here before computers and is still here today. We must be balanced to make sure that the weight we put on the things we measure is in line with the weight we put on the things we cannot measure but can feel and see if we get out into the market place. Keeping strong people motivated will pay big dividends to any company. The bottom line is a manager should not expect anything from his people that he would not do.

A blow up can be a good thing

At first thought, an argument or a strong disagreement might seem to be not good or even unprofessional, but I think a good blow up might be a good thing on occasion. It is very important to communicate in any type of relationship and business is a very important relationship between the people that work together every day. Because human nature makes it hard to agree to disagree, I have seen people work together for years that simply do not ever argue or blow up at each other but always talk behind the others back about whatever they might not agree on. I say get it out and if it takes an argument to get it out, my thought is "let's have at it" because at the end of the day, most often things are better. Honest communication is vital for people to be able to work together and build a healthy culture.

Lessons learned during the last 30 years in business

1) The corporate world can be more perception driven than reality driven. A dangerous practice and the number one cause of the corporate collapse at the turn of this century.

2) Managing down is the only direction that a corporation should be concerned about. A person doing a good job is the only way any employee should be concerned about managing up.

3) Honesty and integrity is the best way to build a strong business team.

4) Politics are too important in most companies. Can you imagine playing politics and starting football players that are not as good as the players on the bench?

5) Weekly management meetings to review what is expected and to FOLLOW up on what has been accomplished are absolutely necessary.

6) Businesses make things too difficult and complex. Use common sense for best results.

7) The only way to teach people new ideas and new ways to do things is to repeat what you want for a minimum of 21 days until they become a habit.

8) The best use of a computer is to use it to help you get organized. Remember, people are not perfect but computers are.

9) Limit the use of e-mails to necessary communication only. Quit using e-mails to put the monkey on someone else's back or because you think you need to "manage" up better.

Lessons learned during the last 30 years in business (Cont'd)

10) One receives in return exactly what one gives out to others.

11) One cannot fool his associates for long; over time opinions are formed based on ones effort, ability and work ethic.

12) Most folks want to give a full day's work and actually feel bad when they do not.

13) The working climate within any company benefits directly from having a respectful, peaceful win – win attitude.

14) The crème will rise to the top. One must have patience.

15) The true value of any business manager is directly proportionate to the positive influence he or she has over the people within the scope of their responsibility.

16) Every person needs a mission statement to review each day to stay focused on his or her priorities.

17) Often in the corporate world, people that are followers are placed in positions of leadership.

Learning and Getting Better is a Life Long Challenge
"Mind your own business."

When you are younger do not waste all your energy partying or going to the gym every extra minute. Look for an alternative income. I was an example of a young man who worked hard for my company (NDC) but also enjoyed physical exercise. At 26 years old, it dawned on me to do something on the weekends that would make money and give me a good work out at the same time. The tree cutting business was a perfect fit. My friend, Keith Harris, who played football at Georgia and I started our business.

We went on to make extra income for the next five years cutting trees on the weekends. I was transferred from Atlanta to Jacksonville, Florida in 1982, or I might still be in the tree cutting business.

From 1982 until 1987, one hundred percent of my time was put towards learning and working in a new position for NDC. One must always make sure their #1 job is complete before starting another venture. One can start a second venture once the # 1 job is satisfied. Using balance is always the key to success.

In 1990, I began working weekends developing real estate skills. Driving through different neighborhoods every Saturday and Sunday learning about home property values took a big effort. Making appointments to go see houses every week was time consuming. I didn't buy any houses for a couple of years but did become one of the best-educated real estate folks in Jacksonville, Florida. Knowing house values was knowledge needed to begin a weekend business career that would pay big dividends in the future.

After majoring in Real Estate at the University of Georgia, it was time to use this knowledge

After a divorce in 1990, I was broke. I had a child support payment and for a two-year period had an alimony payment. I was happy to pay both because my children have always been the center of my life and my ex-wife needed some help to get back on her feet. I had a nice job, but at the end of the day did not have much to live off of. I received a good education in Real Estate at the University of Georgia. Our 40's are the transition years between being younger and older and the decade most folks make the most money. It was time for me to start "transitioning."

I learned from my college days the return on renting a home could be incredible. There were five things to consider. 1) What percent increase were the homes in the desired area going up? 2)

How much mortgage principle would be paid down by the tenant's rental income in a year? 3) What would my tax break be each year for owning a rental house? 4) What type of effort or time would the business take? Would it be worth it? 5) How close would the rental income be to covering the mortgage amount?

I was ready and fired up to get going in what looked like a great second business. Every person I talked to about what I wanted to do could not have been more discouraging. Some of the responses I received were: "Do you know how hard it is to rent homes?" "Have you heard of the horror stories of what renters do to your rental home?" "You will never have the time to make any real money and the hassle will be much worse than the return on your investment." "Be careful because you can lose a lot of money if you don't do it right." "I would never do that." "Have you ever tried to evict someone from a home? It's impossible." My best friend in Atlanta has made millions of dollars in his very successful business and even he was negative.

I loved the no-sayers because it reminded me a lot of playing football. Every one has an opinion or attitude, but the only real opinion or attitude that counts is your own. My goal at 40 years old was to have one home to live in and six rental homes to receive old age income; all paid for by the time I would retire. My plan was to buy and sell some homes and keep the best homes for rental income later in life. In the past 14 years, I have accomplished my goal. I am on schedule to have these homes paid off by retirement age.

Fourteen years ago at 40 years old, sitting on the bench was not an option. Sitting on the bench should never be an option. Losing is better than not trying. The success most people accomplish is because of a positive attitude and a refusal to let other people's negative influence effect them (sports or business). People that tell others what they cannot do are bad leaders and should never be listened to.

The people that told me how hard renting homes would be and how much time it would take were wrong. The Real Estate business is a lot of fun and rewarding.

"Obstacles are those frightful things you see
when you take your eyes off your goal."

Life's Lessons Learned

1) The definition of a manager should be changed to be synonymous with a Coach/Teacher/Mentor. Perhaps we should change job titles from sales manager to sales coach.
2) We all need Healthy competition in our lives.
3) Spinning in business is very unhealthy in the long term.
4) Act on your thoughts or beliefs now because it will be too late soon.
5) The team is always more important and more productive than any single individual.
6) One's instinct usually makes the difference in winning or losing.
7) The things we measure in business are less important than the things we cannot or do not measure.
8) Computers are perfect and people are not.

Chapter Nine

The Ivory Tower Syndrome

The definition of "the Ivory Tower Syndrome" is when one puts themselves in a place above others. They are in a position to influence or lead and then distance themselves from the clear communication that is necessary for any person or company to grow and improve. Over the years many companies do not reach their full potential or fail because the top management of the company gets into the Ivory Tower Syndrome.

Ivory Tower Syndrome symptoms:

1. Top management loses touch with their most important people because they refuse to communicate with them. Sometimes top management only communicates with other top management.
    a. What if a particular manager is not feeding the top people the correct information? I have encountered many insecure managers who are centered on keeping their job and not on the success or failure of the company.

b. What if a particular manager does not like a person who is productive? The feed back on this productive person may not be as good as he deserves.

2. Listening skills usually deteriorate considerably
    a. Some people who rise to big positions think they know everything and begin to lose listening skills

3. Communication deteriorates
    a. Too high up to walk around and talk to the common man.
    b. Sometimes communication loses intended direction when it is delivered one or two levels down.

4. Leading a team by example has to start at the top.
    a. George Jenkins, founder of Publix Super Markets, is one of the greatest retailers in our country's history and he never forgot his roots.
    b. Mr. Jenkins always got out in the market to talk to his employees. People feel respected when the top person shows them this type of attention.

Misconceptions in business

Spinning at the expense of the truth has become the norm in today's society. Examples:

1) How can we believe anything that politicians tell us today?
2) People do bad things and then hire an attorney to "spin" the truth.
3) The business world today is full of people that have learned to spin things to make themselves look better.

Many of these folks have reached very high levels even though they do not have the skills to lead / teach / coach others. The term "empty suit" has been around for a while, but the past several years have proven that we have more empty suits in today's business world than ever before. In today's world of spin, perception is no longer reality and I think most of us have a passion for reality.

"Recent allegations on wall street of breaches of trust or even legality, if true, could begin to undermine the very basis on which the world's greatest financial markets thrive."

"After the revelations of corporate malfeasance, the market punished the stock prices of those corporations whose behaviors had cast doubt on the reliability of their reputations."

"I hope and anticipate that trust and integrity again will be amply rewarded in the marketplace as they were in earlier generations. There is no better antidote for the business and financial transgressions of recent years."

Chairman Alan Greenspan
Jacksonville, FL
Times Union 4/17/04

Things people should strive to achieve in business
"Yes I can"

1) A 100% effort.
2) Integrity and Honesty.
3) Reality not perception.
4) A strong leader, mentor and teacher.
5) A person that walks the walk (a leader by example).
6) A common sense, keep it simple person.
7) A good communicator.
8) A person that understands and is centered on mutual respect (expect the same respect that you give someone).
9) A person that understands, "the person makes the title important, the title never makes the person important."

"Be nice to people on your way up because you will meet them on your way down."

Chapter Ten

Attitude as we age
"Yes I can"

Our attitudes and our minds change as we age. We live the first half of our <u>adult</u> lives that last from 18 to 40 years old then we have a 10 year transitional period from 40 to 49 years old and then we live the second half of our adult lives that will last from 50 until we part this world.

The first half of our adult life, our minds are centered on different things than what our minds are centered on the second half of our adult life as follows:

1. Me vs family, friends and others
2. Partying vs responsibility
3. Learning how to compete in the business world
4. Learning how to make it on our own financially, socially, spiritually, mentally and physically
5. Other's opinions of us
6. Appearance to others and ourselves
7. Strength as it relates to our body
8. Athletic competition
9. Money
10. We are concerned or worried about things we have no control over
11. The opposite sex
12. Being right is more important than being happy

In our 20's we are carefree and try everything. Fun is the most important thing in life. In our 30's we begin to learn business, we take on more responsibility, we start to get a little more balanced.

We begin to mellow at 40 years old and we begin a changing process for the next 9 years. We begin to see our self as mortal. We are looking 50 years old straight in the face. We get a wake up call. We begin to feel the physical stress of aging. We get more focused on where we are headed in our business life. We begin to review our successes and our failures more realistically. We try to make as much money as possible. Our 40's can be very productive income years.

When we turn 50 years old, we emotionally and psycho-logically make a big change. It just happens and we do not have a lot of control over it. Our mind ages as our body ages but there is one big difference in the ageing process between our mind and our body. As we get older, we find out our mind can get better. What we were centered on prior to our 10-year transition has changed in a big way. We have a choice to make, keep trying to be as young physically as we used to be and really get frustrated or become more mental and enjoy things we never thought we could enjoy, by choosing the mental improvement route we can be happy and we can look forward to what we might learn as we age. We do become centered on different things after 50 than we were before 40 as follows:

1) Our family is the #1 priority in life.
2) Our friends are a close #2 to our family and in reality become part of our family.
3) Being responsible is very important to most of us and partying is not important at all.
4) The stress of learning how to compete in the business world is over.
5) The stress of learning how to make it on our own has been learned.

      a. Financially

      b. Socially

      c. Spiritually

      d. Mentally

      e. Physically

6) Others opinions of us are much less important than our opinions of our selves.

7) Looks are not as important.

8) Strength as it relates to our body pales in comparison to strength as it relates to our mind.

9) Athletic competition is fun but not as competitive.

10) We need enough money to be secure but our family, our friends, our health and happiness is more important than money.

11) We are concerned with or worry about things that we do have control over and can change or influence.

12) We look at and view the opposite sex with more respect.

13) Being right is not as important as being happy.

The bottom line is if we are lucky enough to realize during our 40's when a person is young, he will have a physical advantage but when a person gets older, he can have a mental advantage; we can live a happy, fulfilled life. After all, "the power of the mind is much greater than the power of the body."

God Bless Coach Creel, Coach Blackwell, Coach Dooley and Coach Russell and although you might not be around, your influence is ever lasting.

Be A Winner

"Our daily actions are the result of good or bad habits, winning habits learned from sports guarantee success"

* Always give credit where credit is due.
* Center on bringing the average of the Team to a high level.
* Lead by Example.
* Mutual Respect is the only long Term Respect.
* Honesty plus Integrity = Team.
* Preparation = Confidence = Winning.
* Cultures will vary but all people have the same Human Nature.
* Work ethic – out work your competition.
* Attitude always makes the difference in Winning or Losing.
* Coachable People have a chance to reach their full potential
* Don't ever be intimidated, don't ever back down, make your competition earn everything they get and if you win or lose, live with it.
* Personality will make or break most people. Have fun along the way.
* Life is full of failures and how you handle those failures shows your true character.
* Every Individual success is the Result of a Team effort.